Modern protein-packed recipes for every day

The PANEER COOKBOOK

RIYA PATEL

ALL THE AUNTIES

K

For 'All The Aunties' - Sima, Madhu and Kusum - without whom this business wouldn't exist.

First published in Great Britain in 2026 by Kyle, an imprint of
Octopus Publishing Group Ltd
Carmelite House
50 Victoria Embankment
London EC4Y 0DZ
www.octopusbooks.co.uk

An Hachette UK Company
www.hachette.co.uk

The authorized representative in the EEA is Hachette Ireland,
8 Castlecourt Centre, Dublin 15, D15 XTP3, Ireland
(email: info@hbgi.ie)

Additional picture credits: iStock/Daria Khivrenko; happyfoto

Distributed in the US by Hachette Book Group
1290 Avenue of the Americas 4th and 5th Floors
New York, NY 10104

Distributed in Canada by Canadian Manda Group
664 Annette Street Toronto, Ontario M6S 2C8

ISBN 9781804194263
eISBN 9781804194287

A CIP catalogue record for this book is available from the British Library.

Printed and bound in China

10 9 8 7 6 5 4 3 2 1

Publisher: Joanna Copestick
Art Director: Jaz Bahra
Editor: Rosie Hilton
Copyeditor: Emma Clegg
Photographer: Kris Kirkham
Food Stylist: Sonali Shah
Props Stylist: Davina Maji
Senior Production Manager: Peter Hunt

CONTENTS

INTRODUCTION

WHAT'S THE DEAL WITH PANEER?

Whenever I tell people I run a paneer business (or, depending on the day, a 'cheese business') the first question is always the same: why?

Selling paneer wasn't always my ambition – but working in food was. And when I saw Indian ingredients, such as paneer, so often relegated to the 'ethnic' aisle in supermarkets, misunderstood and mispositioned, I thought, 'If halloumi can soar, why can't paneer?'

But this intent is more than just repositioning an underserved ingredient; it is about sharing the amazing ingredients that Indian cuisine is centred around. Miso and tofu have migrated across cuisines, and Indian ingredients can too. This is the joy of living in an increasingly globalized society. Indian food is far more than curry (although of course we do love a good curry).

Walking through supermarket aisles, I was often deflated by how little Indian food I'd actually buy. It all felt tired and stuck in the past, and didn't reflect the food I grew up eating, or the breadth of Indian ingredients. They had been commoditized for the masses, designed for a long shelf life, and stripped of the love these foods are meant to carry. For me, food was always an experience – from start to finish.

This realization led me to hosting supper clubs in London, where I served family dishes. They were largely vegetarian, celebrated seasonal ingredients and, of course, featured paneer. My guests came from a range of backgrounds but they had one thing in common: they loved paneer. Most of them had never thought to cook with it, and even if they had entertained the idea, they wouldn't have been able to find it. I decided in that moment that I was going to make it myself, and with the same love my mum had always put into it.

Two years on from that first supper club, here is our family company, All the Aunties. Stocked nationwide, we are one step closer to bringing paneer to the people.

FOOD, FEEDING AND FAMILY

All the Aunties was born out of my desire to share my family's story through the food that I adore. Through adversity, necessity and joy, food has been a constant love of my life.

I grew up in a family where three generations lived outside India, sometimes by choice, but often not. Like much of the diaspora, they moved from India to East Africa before eventually being displaced again to the UK. Forced to build a new life from scratch somewhere new, it was a common story.

My family came from East Africa having worked as engineers and doctors. When they moved to the UK and US respectively, they worked 12-hour days, lived humbly and gave everything to their children.

Through it all, food played an important role in helping us cling on to our culture, heritage and identity. Food was a language shaped by culture and context. Feeding our family was how we said 'I love you'. Breaking rotli (as roti are called in Gujarat) over a meal was how my grandparents made friends, how cultures assimilated and bonds were formed.

As people, even where we don't share a mother tongue, we can always share the universal language of food.

ALL THE AUNTIES
PANEER
ALL THE AUNTIES
PANEER
GARLIC & HERB
GRILL - FRY - CRUMBLE - SNACK
ALL THE AUNTIES
PANEER
THE ORIGINAL
GRILL - FRY - CRUMBLE - SNACK
ALL THE AUNTIES
PANEER
ALL THE AUNTIES
PANEER
PANEER

MEET THE AUNTIES

There is a wonderful thing called 'aunty culture'. In many communities, it's a sign of affection and respect for older women. For most of us, the word 'aunty' simply feels like home – it evokes a vivid sense of belonging.

They say it takes a village to raise a child, and I've never felt anything to be more true. I was raised by a community of women who fed and nurtured me, taught me to be a generous and decent human being and also showed me the proper way around a kitchen. There were no measuring cups, no scales and no teaspoons; it was about feeling and tasting your way through.

If you are at Aunty's house, you're almost certainly being overfed, being given unsolicited advice, being told you must come back if you're ever hungry, leaving with a doggy bag...and getting set up with their friend's son.

In building the All the Aunties brand, I wanted to put the women of my family, our hidden heroes, front and centre – giving them the time, space and platform they so deserve. Here is an introduction to each of them.

Sima Aunty

I have a confession. Sima is actually my mum and my co-founder Jack's mother-in-law (he's married to my sister).

Sima grew up in Zambia, was educated in the US and then settled in the UK. Despite working full time, she spoilt the family with home-cooked food every single day. She remains the best cook I know. She collects cookbooks, reads them from front to back on weekend mornings and was making the bold and powerful flavour of *spaghetti all'assassina* (killer spaghetti) years before anyone had even heard of it. She is a true foodie.

Under her watch, we ate spiced monkfish for Christmas dinner, enjoyed homemade dosa for Sunday brunch, and were offered nutritious, delicious Gujarati dishes on weeknights. You can find Sima's Paneer Dosa recipe on page 142 and her famous Tadka Dal with Confit Garlic on page 76.

Sima has always loved feeding people. Such acts of service are definitely her love language, although she would scoff if she heard us say that. Sometimes thinking about what to have for dinner can send a home cook into disarray, even without the pressure of feeding a family of four. Sima made it seem effortless. She is the main driver behind the Patel family's love of food and, crucially, she's the one who taught me how to make paneer from scratch.

Aside from food, Sima is also a lover of film. You'll catch her watching westerns on a Sunday afternoon – probably with a hunk of fresh crusty bread and a chunk of vintage Cheddar. Oh, and there will also be a pile of cookbooks nearby.

Kusum Aunty

I have to confess, again, that Kusum (below) is not my aunty, but my grandma. Kusum grew up in Uganda and was forcibly relocated to the UK during the dictatorship. She wasn't fluent in English, but preparing food was her way of communicating with us. Whenever we visited, the refrigerator would be full of our favourite chocolate, sparkling Rubicon (a fruit-flavoured soft drink) and her famous patra (a very skilled, very delicious Gujarati dish).

She made the thinnest, roundest and softest rotlis and had a wonderfully spiced take on pasta – think cumin seeds and red chilli powder – which we loved.

Kusum was kind and gentle and enjoyed a good dramatic soap opera. She had lost her husband in her fifties and remained the bedrock of our family until her passing in 2023. She was cooking until the end – and some of her food is still in the freezer.

It's been such a joy to delve back into her old recipes, dig out photos and remember her through the greatest of all love languages – food. Some of her dishes feature in this book. I hope you enjoy cooking and eating them just as much as we did (and still do).

Madhu Aunty

Madhu is genuinely the greatest cook we have ever known. Exceptionally skilled, she makes everything from scratch – including bread and yogurt – and she thinks the rest of the family are absolutely terrible cooks.

Putting paneer in a salad is not something Madhu approves of. She is a purist and, to be honest, I do get it. As she put it when I launched All the Aunties: 'She is launching an Indian food business and doesn't even like Indian food.'

To clarify, I *love* Indian food. It just so happened that on this particular occasion I wanted Mexican instead.

After relocating from East Africa, Madhu set up a video shop in the US and eventually settled there to build her family. Food was so integral to maintaining identity, culture and home that she rarely bypassed tradition. She was also an egg-free vegetarian, so when living in the US, finding good options outside the home wasn't always easy.

Madhu is charismatic, loves receiving gifts and is very beautiful – and she knows it. She is Sima's mum (who is my mum, so another grandma!), and much of the food in this book is a homage to Sima and Madhu's style of cooking.

COOKING LIKE AN AUNTY

I hope I have succeeded in getting you to think about two things:

How can I eat at an Aunty's house?
You invite yourself over. That's just how it goes.

How can I cook like an Aunty?
Aunties don't do measurements – they judge with their hands. It comes from years of experience and from that ever-annoying phrase, 'measure with your heart'. I encourage you to channel your inner heart-measurer as you cook from this book. You really can't go too far wrong.

When frying paneer (though it's also wonderful when baked or cooked in curry), it is best to use ghee, mustard oil or a neutral oil. Common examples of neutral oil in the UK include vegetable oil, sunflower oil and rapeseed oil, all of which have a mild flavour and are well suited to everyday cooking.

THE TASTE OF BELONGING

'Diaspora' is a term used to describe the spread of a group of people from their homeland to other areas. People of Indian descent are spread across the world, assimilating into different cultures and communities, in the process creating a rich third culture.

I am a British-Indian. Born in London, the city is my home. Those who have grown up as part of the diaspora often feel they have a foot in two cultures – it can be displacing, but it can also be wonderful. All the Aunties is a homage to this, and I hope that if the idea is familiar to you, you will feel seen in our brand, our stories and our food.

This is a poem I wrote as I was setting up the business – I hope it resonates.

THERE ARE ALSO A FEW PRACTICAL TIPS I'VE PICKED UP ALONG THE WAY:

Use tadkas
Tadkas are unbelievable flavour boosters. They take two minutes to make, can be prepared in advance and in bulk, and can be stored for ages in an airtight container. There are plenty of tadkas in this book (see page 162).

Use moist paneer
Lots of paneer can be dense, rubbery and dry, so be sure to source a good one. If you happen to buy the dense stuff, soak your paneer in hot water for a few minutes before use to soften it.

A 'pinch' means a three-finger pinch
... not the usual two.

Sugar is seasoning
... just as salt is.

Buy ginger-garlic paste
You can make it yourself by combining crushed garlic cloves and grated fresh ginger, but buying it will save you hours, and you can keep blocks of it in your freezer.

Don't be afraid of fat
Ghee and oil are essential to tempering spices and aromatics – they add flavour and depth.

A DISH THAT REMEMBERS

I was born with a passport, not a map,
a scattered lineage of aunties and accents,
uncles with stories stitched in suitcases,
cousins waving from opposite ends of
the equator.

We are spread...like spices spilled,
diaspora by design,
sometimes by choice,
often not.

My name holds syllables softened by strangers.
Too British there, too brown here
a foot in two worlds
and still feeling barefoot.

But the kitchen never asked questions.
I learnt that identity can simmer gently
in mustard seeds popping in hot oil,
in cumin rising like incense,
in my mother's hands shaping dough
as her mother once did
under another sun.

Food tethers me,
a thread of turmeric through every
version of me.
When I feel blurred,
I find clarity
in the smell of home-cooked food,
in recipes that remember,
even when I forget.

PANEER FOR THE PEOPLE

Before you dive into the world of paneer, I want to remind you of one thing: Indian food is much more than curry. The diaspora culture is rich and delicious and so very special. I'd love you to help us on our mission to break paneer out of the curry house by experimenting a little. And if in doubt, Aunty's got plenty of recipes for you.

Making paneer is a labour of love, but it is not difficult. In fact, it is one of the best ways to enjoy this delicious ingredient. You can also swap the paneer used in this book for other proteins, such as tempeh, tofu or even chicken. If you can't find paneer easily where you live, it is simple to make your own. All you need is whole milk and an acid – either lemon juice or vinegar – and cheesecloth or muslin for sieving.

When kept in an airtight container in the refrigerator, paneer will keep for up to three days, although it's best eaten within 24 hours.

Making your own paneer

1 LITRE (1¾ PINTS) MILK MAKES ROUGHLY 100–150G (3½–5½OZ) PANEER (ENOUGH FOR 1–2 SERVINGS).

Each litre of milk requires 2–3 tablespoons of lemon juice or white vinegar.

1. Pour 1 litre (1¾ pints) of milk, or more if scaling up, into a saucepan and heat gently over a medium heat. Stir occasionally to prevent it catching on the bottom.
2. Bring the milk to just below boiling (around 90°C/194°F) – you'll see steam rising and small bubbles forming around the edges.
3. Remove the pan from the heat and slowly stir in 2–3 tablespoons of lemon juice or white vinegar per litre of milk.
4. Gently stir once or twice. The milk should begin to separate into curds, leaving a pale green whey. If it doesn't fully split, add a little more lemon juice or vinegar, one teaspoon at a time.
5. Leave the mixture to sit undisturbed for 10 minutes to allow the curds to fully form.
6. Line a sieve with cheesecloth or muslin and pour the curds and whey through it. Rinse the curds briefly under cold water to remove any lemon or vinegar flavour.
7. Gather the cloth around the curds and squeeze out the excess liquid.
8. Place the wrapped paneer on a plate and compress it with a weight (a heavy pan, books or a tofu press work well). Leave it to compress for 30–60 minutes, depending on how firm you want it – the longer it is pressed, the firmer it will be.
9. Once firm, unwrap and cut into cubes or slices. The paneer is now ready to cook; it's especially delicious when fried until golden.

PICKY BITS

SERVES: 4 • PREP TIME: 20 MINUTES • COOK TIME: 15 MINUTES

Classic Chilli Paneer

A classic for a reason. If you're cooking for someone who's not convinced by paneer, this is the dish that will win them over. Sweet, spicy, tangy and irresistibly pillowy. If you haven't tried it yet, what are you waiting for?

400g (14oz) plain paneer or All the Aunties Cumin, Chilli & Turmeric Paneer, diced
2 tablespoons neutral oil, plus extra for frying
1 red or white onion, cut into 8 segments
6 spring onions, sliced
8 garlic cloves, crushed or finely chopped
5-cm (2-inch) piece of fresh root ginger, finely chopped
2 bell peppers, deseeded and cut into wedges
2 green chillies, slit lengthways (deseed if you want less heat)

FOR THE DRY COATING
3 tablespoons cornflour
2 tablespoons plain flour
1 teaspoon red chilli powder
1 teaspoon chaat masala, or ½ teaspoon ground cumin plus ½ teaspoon ground coriander
1 teaspoon salt
1 teaspoon pepper

FOR THE SAUCE
4 tablespoons soy sauce, a mixture of light and dark
3 tablespoons tomato ketchup
3 tablespoons hot sauce
2 teaspoons clear honey
2 teaspoons white wine or apple cider vinegar
1 teaspoon cornflour
125–250ml (4–8fl oz) water

1 Start by making the dry coating mix. Combine the cornflour, flour and seasonings in a large bowl.

2 Toss the paneer with 1 tablespoon of neutral oil before coating it evenly in the dry batter. Air-fry at 180°C (350°F) for 5–7 minutes, or until golden and crisp. Alternatively, shallow-fry in a nonstick frying pan for 5–7 minutes, turning until crisp on all sides. For a more indulgent option, heat a 5-cm (2-inch) depth of oil in a deep pan until it reaches 180–190°C, then deep-fry the cubes until crisp and golden. Set aside.

3 In a nonstick pan over a medium–high heat, add the remaining tablespoon of oil and fry the onion segments, spring onions, garlic, ginger, peppers and green chillies. Let cook for 3–4 minutes, until aromatic.

4 Meanwhile, make your sauce. Place all the ingredients in a bowl and mix until smooth, adding the water gradually. Add to the onion pan and cook for 2–3 minutes, until the cornflour starts to thicken the mixture, and the sauce looks glossy.

5 Toss the paneer cubes in the sauce over a medium heat for 1–2 minutes, until heated through and evenly coated. Serve immediately.

SERVES: 8-10 (MAKES AROUND 20 PARCELS) • PREP TIME: 25 MINUTES • COOK TIME: 10 MINUTES

Paneer Potli

Little parcels of deliciousness. You'll often find these at weddings and parties, sometimes stuffed with sweetcorn, peas or peppers, but we've kept them simple here. The perfect vehicle for dunking into chutneys and sauces, they are ideal for hosting (and showing off).

2 tablespoons neutral oil, plus extra for brushing and deep-frying
1 teaspoon cumin seeds
1 teaspoon carom seeds (ajwain)
1 red onion, finely chopped
2 green chillies, finely chopped
3 garlic cloves, crushed or finely chopped
3-cm (1-inch) piece fresh root ginger, finely chopped
400g (14oz) paneer, grated or crumbled
1 teaspoon ground cumin
1 teaspoon ground coriander
½–1 teaspoon red chilli powder
½ teaspoon white sugar
Lemon juice, to taste (optional)
4 tablespoons chopped coriander
4 spring onions, finely chopped
20–24 spring roll wrappers
Salt and pepper

1 To make the paneer filling, heat the measured oil in a heavy-based frying pan over a medium heat. Add the cumin and carom seeds and cook until fragrant. Fry for 1 minute before adding the onion, chillies and salt and cook for 1–2 minutes before adding the garlic and ginger.

2 Add the paneer to the pan. Cook for 2–3 minutes until softened.

3 Add the ground spices and sugar, then taste and adjust for seasoning. Lemon juice can be added here, if you like. Garnish with fresh coriander and spring onions. Set aside to cool.

4 To assemble the paneer potli, place one wrapper square on the work surface and spoon 2–3 teaspoons of filling into the centre. Gather the edges up around the filling to form a pouch, brush the sides with water and gently pinch it to seal. Use a thin strip of wrapper to tie the top if needed, and place on a tray. Repeat this step with the remaining wrappers and filling.

5 If using an air-fryer, brush the potlis with oil and air-fry at 180°C (350°F) for 8–10 minutes. Alternatively, heat a 5-cm (2-inch) depth of oil in a deep pan until it reaches 180–190°C, then deep-fry the potlis a few at a time. When crisp and golden, drain on kitchen paper and keep warm while you cook the rest.

6 Serve hot with chutney (see pages 168–9).

SERVES: 4-6 • PREP TIME: 15 MINUTES • COOK TIME: 10 MINUTES

Salt 'n' Pepper Paneer

I absolutely love this spicy, salty, garlicky and deeply aromatic dish. The five spice leaves your mouth watering, while the cornflour coating creates a crisp crust that clings to the spice mix. Paired with the soft paneer inside, it makes for an incredibly moreish snack.

Neutral oil, for frying, plus 2 tablespoons extra for sautéing
400g (14oz) paneer, cut into 2.5-cm (1-inch) cubes
1 red onion, finely chopped
12 garlic cloves, finely chopped
2 red chillies, finely chopped (deseed if you want less heat)
1 green chilli, finely chopped (deseed if you want less heat; optional)
10 spring onions, finely sliced
Sprigs of fresh coriander or Masala Chilli Crisp, to garnish (see page 171; optional)

FOR THE SALT 'N' PEPPER MIX
1 teaspoon sea salt
½ teaspoon white pepper
1 teaspoon black pepper
¾ teaspoon Chinese five-spice
½ teaspoon granulated white sugar

FOR THE PANEER COATING
60g (2¼oz) cornflour
1 teaspoon sea salt
2 teaspoons white, black or mixed pepper
¾ teaspoon Chinese five spice

1. First make the salt and pepper mix: combine all the dry ingredients in a small bowl and set aside.
2. Heat a 5-cm (2-inch) depth of oil in a deep pan or wok and heat over a medium-high heat.
3. Meanwhile, make the paneer coating: mix the cornflour with the salt, pepper and five spice in a large bowl. Working in batches, toss the paneer cubes in the mixture until evenly coated. Shake off any excess flour. Once coated, cook the paneer immediately – don't let it sit in the cornflour.
4. Carefully add the paneer to the hot oil without overcrowding the pan. Fry for 2–3 minutes, turning gently, until crisp on the outside. Drain on kitchen paper, then cook the remaining cubes in the same way.
5. Pour off the frying oil and return the pan to a high heat with 2 tablespoons fresh oil. Add the onion and cook for 1 minute, then push to the side and add the garlic. Cook until golden and crisp, and add the chillies. Stir in the spring onions, reserving some for garnish, and cook for a further 1–2 minutes. The onions should be soft and translucent, and the garlic lightly golden.
6. Add the fried paneer to the pan over a high heat. Sprinkle over half the salt and pepper mixture and toss well. Taste and adjust the seasoning, adding the remainder of the salt and pepper if needed. The paneer should be salty, spicy and very aromatic.
7. Garnish with the reserved spring onions, and the fresh coriander or chilli crisp, if using. Serve immediately while hot and crisp.

SERVES: 4 • PREP TIME: 10 MINUTES • COOK TIME: 10 MINUTES

Buffalo Paneer Nuggets

I have a lot of family in the US, and there are a few food non-negotiables when I visit. Top of the list is buffalo wings – properly saucy, messy and a total guilty pleasure. Even though I've moved away from meat, I still want to recreate that same experience – and these nuggets hit the spot. Crispy, spicy, a little indulgent and best eaten hot.

400g (14oz) paneer
4–6 tablespoons panko breadcrumbs
1 large egg, or 2 medium eggs, beaten
Neutral oil, for brushing or deep-frying

FOR THE COATING
1–2 tablespoons cornflour
½ teaspoon salt
½ teaspoon chilli powder
1 teaspoon garlic powder
1 teaspoon paprika
1 teaspoon pepper
½ teaspoon smoked paprika (optional)

FOR THE BUFFALO SAUCE
2 tablespoons butter
6 tablespoons Frank's RedHot sauce, or another hot sauce of your choice
1 tablespoon clear honey

TO SERVE
Ranch or blue cheese dressing, fresh celery and salty fries

1. Roughly tear the paneer into bite-sized pieces. Tearing gives the paneer a more substantial, meaty texture.
2. Make the coating: stir together the cornflour, salt, chilli powder, garlic powder, paprika and pepper in a bowl. Set aside.
3. Lightly dust each paneer piece with the coating.
4. Dip the paneer into the beaten egg and then into the panko breadcrumbs. Place the coated pieces on a plate and set aside.
5. To make the buffalo sauce, melt the butter, then stir in the hot sauce and honey.
6. Air-fry at 180°C (350°F) for 5–7 minutes, or heat a 5-cm (2-inch) depth of oil in a deep pan until it reaches 180–190°C, then deep-fry the coated paneer pieces for about 3–4 minutes, until golden brown.
7. Transfer the paneer bites to a large mixing bowl and coat them with the buffalo sauce.
8. Serve immediately with a side of ranch or blue cheese dressing, plus celery and salty fries.

SERVES: 4 • PREP TIME: 5 MINUTES • COOK TIME: 15 MINUTES

Sticky Garlic & Gochujang Bites

Garlic, sesame and soy are ingredients that are always knocking about in my pantry, so this is my go-to when I want big flavour in under 10 minutes. Sticky, savoury and endlessly versatile, throw these bites into noodles, pile them onto rice, or tuck them into lettuce cups for something lighter. If you crumble rather than cube the paneer, you can also use the result as a delicious vegetarian alternative to mince.

1–2 tablespoons neutral oil, for frying
400g (14oz) paneer, cut into 2.5-cm (1-inch) cubes

FOR THE GLAZE
3 tablespoons clear honey
5 tablespoons soy sauce
1 tablespoon rice vinegar
1 tablespoon toasted sesame oil
1 tablespoon gochujang
½–¾ teaspoons cornflour
2–3 tablespoons water
1 tablespoon neutral oil
6 garlic cloves, crushed or finely chopped

TO FINISH
2 tablespoons sesame seeds
2 spring onions, finely sliced
Crushed roasted peanuts
Red chilli, finely sliced (deseed if you want less heat)
Small handful of coriander, finely chopped
Squeeze of lime juice

TO SERVE
Steamed rice and greens, or tuck the bites into lettuce cups

1. Place the neutral oil in a heavy-based frying pan over a medium heat. When hot, fry the paneer until crisp and golden on all sides. Set aside.
2. Whisk the the glaze ingredients (apart from the oil and garlic) in a bowl until smooth. Heat the oil over a medium heat in the empty paneer pan. Add the garlic and cook for 30 seconds, until fragrant. Pour in the glaze and simmer for 3–4 minutes, stirring frequently, until glossy and thickened. If it's too salty, add a touch more water.
3. Add the crispy paneer to the pan and toss gently to coat. Scatter over the sesame seeds, spring onions, crushed peanuts and red chillies. Finish with the chopped coriander and a squeeze of lime.
4. Serve immediately while hot and crisp, with steamed rice and greens. Alternatively, tuck the bites into crisp lettuce cups.

SERVES: 4 • PREP TIME: 5 MINUTES • COOK TIME: 10 MINUTES

Keralan Pepper Fry

Here's my take on a Keralan pepper fry, a dish known for its use of black pepper, curry leaves and warming spices. Traditionally made with meat, the magic here is in the punchy masala sauce that clings to everything in the pan. The paneer soaks it all up beautifully while staying soft and satisfying.

400g (14oz) paneer, cut into 2.5-cm (1-inch) cubes
1 tablespoon cornflour
½ teaspoon sea salt
Neutral oil, for frying

FOR THE PEPPER FRY
2 tablespoons coconut or neutral oil
2 teaspoons black mustard seeds
2 sprigs of curry leaves (10–15 dried leaves)
1 teaspoon fennel seeds, lightly crushed
1 teaspoon cumin seeds, lightly crushed
1 red onion, thinly sliced
8 garlic cloves, crushed or finely chopped
5-cm (2-inch) piece of root ginger, finely chopped
3 green chillies, slit lengthways (deseed if you want less heat)
3 teaspoons black pepper
1 teaspoon ground coriander
1 teaspoon ground cumin
¼ teaspoon ground turmeric
1–2 tablespoons soy sauce or tamarind sauce
1–2 tablespoons lemon juice
Salt

1. Toss the paneer in a bowl with the cornflour and salt.
2. Heat a shallow layer of oil in a heavy-based frying pan over a medium–high heat and fry the paneer until lightly golden and crisp on all sides. This will take a few minutes, so be patient, it will come together. Remove and set aside.
3. Wipe out the pan, add the coconut oil and return it to the heat. Add the mustard seeds and let them pop (stand back as you do this), then add the curry leaves. After a minute or two add the fennel and cumin seeds. Toast until aromatic, being careful not to burn them.
4. Add the onion and cook for 5–6 minutes, until soft and lightly caramelized. Stir in the garlic, ginger and green chillies and cook for 1–2 minutes until fragrant.
5. Add the black pepper, coriander, cumin and turmeric. Cook for 30 seconds, stirring constantly.
6. Return the paneer to the pan and toss well to coat in the spices. Add the soy or tamarind sauce and cook for 2–3 minutes, letting the paneer take on colour.
7. Sprinkle with the lemon juice and add salt, if needed.
8. Serve this fry on its own as a starter, or atop rice with pickles and sambar (see page 170) as a main.

SERVES: 4–6 • PREP TIME: 15 MINUTES • COOK TIME: 10 MINUTES

Nachodums

Nachodums are what happen when two of my favourite snack worlds collide – Mexican nachos and Indian chaat. Mini poppadoms are piled high with all the good stuff: crumbled mango-glazed paneer, chutneys, yogurt, something fresh, something spicy and a good bit of crunch. A slightly lighter alternative to classic nachos, they are low effort, high reward, and just as lovely to look at as they are to eat.

1 tablespoon neutral oil
200g (7oz) paneer, crumbled
2 tablespoons Mango Chutney (see page 169)
½ teaspoon chaat masala (optional), plus extra to garnish
Pinch of chilli powder (optional)
85g (3oz) mini poppadums
Salt

FOR THE RAITA
200g (7oz) thick Greek yogurt
2 tablespoons deseeded cucumber, finely diced
1 tablespoon lemon juice
Pinch of salt
Pinch of roasted cumin powder

FOR THE TOMATO 'SALSA'
2 tomatoes, finely chopped
¼ small red onion, very finely chopped
1 green chilli, very finely chopped (deseed if you want less heat), or 4–5 pickled jalapeños, chopped
2 tablespoons lime juice (reduce or omit if using pickled jalapeños)
Pinch of salt
1 tablespoon chopped coriander

TO FINISH
Coriander Chutney and Tamarind Chutney (see page 168)
Fresh pomegranate seeds
Sprigs of fresh coriander

1. Heat the oil in a heavy-based frying pan over a medium heat. Add the paneer and warm gently for 2–3 minutes.
2. Stir in the mango chutney, chaat masala and chilli powder, if using. Toss together until the paneer is lightly glazed and warmed through. Taste and add a small pinch of salt, if needed. Remove from the heat – the mixture should be sticky but not wet.
3. For the raita, mix the yogurt with the cucumber, lemon juice, salt and roasted cumin powder until well combined. The result should be thick, cooling and slightly tangy.
4. Mix the tomato salsa ingredients together in a small bowl and set aside.
5. To assemble the dish, arrange the mini poppadums on a large platter in a single layer. Spoon small mounds of warm mango-glazed paneer into each one. Add a little tomato 'salsa' and drizzle the raita lightly over the top. Drizzle with ribbons of coriander chutney and tamarind chutney, then sprinkle with pomegranate seeds, fresh coriander and some chaat masala.
6. Serve immediately so the poppadums remain crisp.

SERVES: 4–6 • PREP TIME: 5 MINUTES • COOK TIME: 10 MINUTES

Honey & Sriracha Bites

This is one of my first-ever recipes, and the dish to make when introducing paneer to first-timers. It is sweet, spicy, garlicky – and brilliant tossed through grains with a good drizzle of Kewpie mayo.

1 tablespoon neutral oil
400g (14oz) paneer, cut into 2.5-cm (1-inch) cubes
½ teaspoon salt
1½ tablespoons Sriracha (chilli sauce)
1 teaspoon garlic granules or 2 garlic cloves, chopped or grated
2 tablespoons clear honey

TO SERVE
Sprinkle of sesame seeds and spring onions as a starter
Green salad for a light lunch
Sticky rice as a main

1 Heat the oil in a heavy-based nonstick pan over a medium heat. Add the paneer and fry with the salt until golden on all sides.

2 Add the Sriracha, garlic granules and honey to the pan and toss for 1–2 minutes until the honey turns glossy and caramelizes around the paneer. Cook for another 1–2 minutes, until deeply golden with a caramelized crust.

3 Serve with any of the suggested accompaniments.

SERVES: 4 • PREP TIME: 5 MINUTES • COOK TIME: 10 MINUTES

Paneer Nuggets

These give chicken nuggets a run for their money. Great for kids and adults, they freeze and reheat beautifully, so it's always worth having a batch on standby. Serve with ketchup or curry sauce and mayo, fries on the side.

400g (14oz) paneer, torn into bite-sized pieces
120g (4¼oz) plain flour
1 teaspoon paprika
1 teaspoon garlic powder
1 teaspoon onion powder
1½ teaspoons salt
½ teaspoon pepper
2 large eggs or 175ml (6fl oz) buttermilk
50–65g (1¾–2¼oz) panko breadcrumbs, cornflakes or sev (chickpea noodles), crushed
Neutral oil, for brushing or deep-frying

TO SERVE
Tomato ketchup or curry sauce
Mayo
Chips

1. If you are using the oven, preheat it to 220°C (425°F), Gas Mark 7.
2. Pat the paneer completely dry with kitchen paper, then toss with the salt and black pepper. Set aside while you prepare the coatings.
3. In one shallow bowl, combine the flour, paprika, garlic powder, onion powder, salt and pepper.
4. In a second bowl, whisk the eggs until smooth, or pour in the buttermilk.
5. Place the panko, cornflakes or sev in a third bowl, lightly crushing them between your fingers.
6. Working in batches, coat the paneer first in the flour mixture, shaking off any excess. Dip into the egg or buttermilk, allowing the excess to drip away, then press firmly into the crumbs so the coating sticks to all sides. Arrange the coated nuggets on a tray lined with baking paper and leave to rest for 10 minutes to help the coating set.
7. To cook in an air-fryer, lightly brush the nuggets with oil. Cook for 10–12 minutes at 190°C (375°F), turning halfway through, until the nuggets are deeply golden and crisp.
8. To bake in the oven, brush the nuggets lightly with oil and bake for 15–18 minutes, turning once, until deeply golden and crunchy.
9. To deep-fry, heat a 5-cm (2-inch) depth of oil in a deep pan until it reaches 180–190°C, then fry the nuggets for 2–3 minutes, until evenly golden. Drain on kitchen paper.
10. Serve immediately while hot and crisp with tomato ketchup or curry sauce and, of course, some chips.

SERVES: 4 • PREP TIME: 5 MINUTES • COOK TIME: 20 MINUTES

Paneer 65 (-ish)

Chicken 65 is a classic South Indian dish. It's not clear where the '65' comes from, but the common origin story is that it most likely refers to 1965, the year the dish was developed at the Buhari Hotel in Chennai. Heavy on aromatics and curry leaves, it is tangy, fiery and earthy. While this isn't an authentic 65 (the soy and ketchup take this into more Indo-Chinese territory), it's certainly inspired by those classic flavours. And it's delicious.

2 tablespoons cornflour
1 tablespoon plain flour
2 teaspoons crushed or grated ginger
2 teaspoons crushed or grated garlic
½ teaspoon cumin seeds
1 teaspoon red chilli powder
½ teaspoon ground turmeric
1 teaspoon ground cumin
1 teaspoon garam masala
1 teaspoon pepper
400g (14oz) 'All the Aunties Cumin, Chilli & Turmeric Paneer', cut into bite-sized cubes
Salt, to taste

FOR THE SAUCE
1–2 tablespoons neutral oil
4 garlic cloves, finely chopped
3 green chillies, sliced (deseed if you want less heat)
2 sprigs of curry leaves (10–12 leaves)
3 tablespoons soy sauce
1½ tablespoons Maggi Hot & Sweet Sauce (or tomato ketchup and sweet chilli sauce)

TO SERVE
2 tablespoons lemon juice
Spring onions, finely sliced
Fresh coriander, chopped

1 Preheat the oven to 200°C (400°F), Gas Mark 6.

2 Mix the cornflour, plain flour, ginger, garlic, spices and salt with just enough water (around 2 tablespoons) to make a thick batter. You want it to cling to the paneer, not drip off.

3 Add the paneer and stir well. Let it rest here for a few minutes.

4 Spread the paneer on a tray lined with baking paper and roast for about 20 minutes, turning once halfway through, until crisp and lightly golden. If air-frying, cook for 10–12 minutes at 180°C, turning halfway through. You can also pan-fry it using a nonstick pan over a medium heat for a more even crust – around 2 minutes on each side.

5 While the paneer cooks, prepare the sauce. Heat the oil in a pan and fry the garlic, chillies and curry leaves, until fragrant and lightly sizzling.

6 When the paneer is ready, add the soy sauce and hot sauce to the pan and let them bubble briefly.

7 Tip in the paneer and toss quickly so everything is coated and the paneer stays crisp.

8 Sprinkle with the lemon juice, spring onions and coriander before serving.

SERVES: 2–3 • PREP TIME: 15 MINUTES • COOK TIME: 10 MINUTES

Paneer Chaat

Chaat is one of the great joys of Indian street food. It comes in many forms, from samosas and puris to sandwiches and crisps. The core elements stay the same: yogurt, coriander chutney, tamarind chutney, chaat masala, sev, red onion and coriander. From there, it's all about mix and match - chickpeas, potatoes, paneer...

This version is a bit of a showstopper. It's quick to put together and perfect for sharing. Try serving it alongside some breads as a loaded dip.

1–2 tablespoons neutral oil
200g (7oz) All the Aunties Cumin, Chilli & Turmeric Paneer, diced
1 tablespoon chaat masala (to taste)
200g (7oz) thick yogurt
3 tablespoons Tamarind Chutney **(see page 168)**
3 tablespoons Coriander Chutney **(see page 168)**

TO SERVE
50g (1¾oz) sev (chickpea noodles), crumbled
Small handful of red onion, finely chopped
50g (1¾oz) pomegranate seeds
Small handful of coriander, finely chopped

1 Heat the oil in a heavy-based frying pan over a medium heat and fry the paneer until golden on all sides. Proper colour is key – it makes all the difference.

2 Turn off the heat and immediately sprinkle over the chaat masala, tossing gently to coat evenly.

3 Spoon the yogurt onto a serving plate to form a base layer. Drizzle the tamarind and coriander chutneys over the yogurt, then add the warm paneer and finish with another light drizzle of chutney.

4 Sprinkle generously with sev, red onion, pomegranate seeds and fresh coriander for crunch and freshness.

SERVES: 4–6 • PREP TIME: 20 MINUTES • COOK TIME: 20 MINUTES

Paneer & Courgette Pakoras

These are my mum's famous pakoras. At every party or family gathering, there would be a batch frying away in the kitchen. I used to make them for school fairs and was embarrassingly proud of the reaction they got. To this day, friends and family still ask for them. Best eaten fresh, hot and crisp – with coriander chutney on the side.

250g (9oz) grated courgette (or mix and match with carrot, raw beetroot, broccoli, spinach)
200g (7oz) grated or crumbled paneer (All the Aunties Cumin, Chilli & Turmeric Paneer works well)
½ tablespoon fennel seeds
2 teaspoons ground cumin
2 teaspoons garam masala
1 teaspoon ground turmeric
1 teaspoon red chilli powder
50g (1¾oz) finely chopped coriander
1 tablespoon finely chopped green chilli (deseed if you want less heat)
½ teaspoon asafoetida
125g (4½oz) yogurt
90g (3¼oz) cornflour
240g (8½oz) chickpea flour
1 teaspoon baking powder
1½–2 teaspoons salt
375ml (12 ½fl oz) ice-cold water
Neutral oil, for frying
Coriander Chutney, to serve (see page 168)

1. Put everything, apart from the oil and chutney, into a large bowl and mix gently, taking care not to beat the batter too vigorously. Set aside for a few minutes so the baking powder can wake up.
2. Add the ice-cold water, a tablespoon at a time, until you have a loose, pancake-style batter that you can drop into oil. If it feels too liquid, add a bit more flour.
3. Heat a 5-cm (2-inch) depth of oil in a deep pan over a medium heat. When hot enough, a small bit of batter should float and start frying straight away. If it sinks, heat the oil for another minute.
4. Carefully drop the batter into the pan in small handfuls, and fry for 2–3 minutes on each side, until golden and crisp. You can do a trial pakora first. If it comes out too dense, add some liquid and drop into the oil in smaller handfuls to ensure they cook thoroughly.
5. Lift the pakoras out, let them drain briefly, and serve hot with the chutney.

SERVES: 2–4 • PREP TIME: 5 MINUTES • COOK TIME: 10 MINUTES

Sticky Mango Chutney-glazed Paneer

This isn't so much a recipe as a simple combination you can add to your rotation. I toss paneer in mango chutney on a weekly basis – it becomes beautifully caramelized on the outside, slightly sticky and soft on the inside. I usually add it to salads or just tuck it into a sandwich with some lettuce, cucumber and onion. It's easy, delicious and children love it.

1 tablespoon neutral oil
200g (7oz) paneer, cubed
1 tablespoon Mango Chutney (see page 169)
¼ teaspoon sea salt (or to taste)

TO SERVE
Crispy onions
Fresh coriander, roughly chopped
Raita (see page 167)

1 Heat the oil in a heavy-based frying pan over a medium heat. Add the paneer in a single layer and fry for around 4 minutes, turning occasionally, until golden on all sides.

2 Add the mango chutney and salt along with 1 tablespoon of water and cook for 2–3 minutes, stirring gently until the paneer is evenly coated and the chutney caramelizes in the pan. If the glaze becomes too thick, add a small splash of water to loosen. The cubes should be sticky and caramelized when ready.

3 Transfer to a serving plate and garnish with crispy onions and coriander. Serve immediately with the raita.

SERVES: 8 • PREP TIME: 20 MINUTES • COOK TIME: 10 MINUTES

Za'atar-crusted Paneer

This recipe is inspired by Ottolenghi, and is a wonderful and different way to enjoy paneer. The cheese carries the za'atar perfectly, with creamy hummus and a tangy roasted red pepper sauce. It's a pretty fantastic bite.

Neutral oil, for brushing or deep-frying
400g (14oz) paneer torn into 2.5-cm (1-inch) chunks

FOR THE PANEER COATING
2 tablespoons cornflour
1 teaspoon salt
¼ teaspoon black pepper
2 eggs, beaten
2½ tablespoons za'atar
6 tablespoons panko breadcrumbs

FOR THE HUMMUS
1 x 400g (14oz) can chickpeas, drained
2 tablespoons tahini
1 garlic clove
2 tablespoons lemon juice, plus some lemon zest
½–1 teaspoon ground cumin
3–4 tablespoons olive oil
Salt, to taste

FOR THE SAUCE
2 large roasted red peppers (from a jar), drained
1 tablespoon red wine vinegar
1 teaspoon clear honey
1 small garlic clove
2 tablespoons olive oil
Pinch of chilli flakes
Salt and pepper

TO FINISH
Olive oil
Za'atar
Fresh parsley, roughly chopped
Pomegranate seeds (optional)
Flaked almonds (optional)

1 First make the hummus: blend the chickpeas, tahini, garlic, lemon juice and zest, cumin, olive oil and salt in a blender or food processor. Add 2–4 tablespoons of ice-cold water, a bit at a time, until the hummus is smooth, creamy and spreadable. Taste and adjust the seasoning.

2 To make the red peper sauce, blend all the ingredients for it until smooth but still slightly textured. It should be spoonable and vibrant.

3 Prepare the paneer coating. Mix the cornflour, salt and black pepper. Place the beaten eggs in a second bowl. In a third bowl mix the za'atar and panko breadcrumbs.

4 Press the paneer first into the cornflour mixture, shaking off any excess. Dip into the beaten egg, then press into the za'atar mixture so the pieces are well coated. Set aside for 5 minutes to help the coating adhere.

5 If air-frying the paneer, brush lightly with oil then cook at 190°C (375°F) for 8–10 minutes, turning halfway through. For deep-frying, heat a 5-cm (2-inch) depth of oil in a deep pan until it reaches 180–190°C, then deep-fry the paneer for 3–4 minutes, until golden.

6 To assemble, spread the hummus generously over a serving platter. Arrange the warm paneer on top, then spoon the red pepper sauce over and around it. Finish with a drizzle of olive oil, a pinch of za'atar and some chopped parsley. Sprinkle with pomegranate seeds and flaked almonds, if you wish.

BURNT BROCCOLI, COURGETTE & BULGUR WHEAT SALAD 43

CRISPY NOODLE SALAD WITH SWEET CHILLI PANEER 44

SUN-DRIED TOMATO, OLIVE & ORZO SALAD 46

CHARRED CORN & AVOCADO SALAD WITH BLACKENED PANEER 47

GRILLED PEACH PANZANELLA WITH HOT-HONEY PANEER 49

KUNG PAO PANEER SALAD WITH PAK CHOI & CRISPY RICE 50

SUPERGREEN GODDESS SALAD 53

BIG SALAD ENERGY

SERVES: 4 AS A MAIN • PREP TIME: 15 MINUTES • COOK TIME: 25 MINUTES

Burnt Broccoli, Courgette & Bulgur Wheat Salad

As a child, I was always suspicious of the broccoli I was served (it was often boiled to oblivion). But when I first had barbecued broccoli, my life was changed. When it's charred, it's pretty much perfect. This can be made in advance for lunch or as a side.

1 head of broccoli, florets separated
1 courgette, sliced into rough chunks
400g (14oz) paneer, sliced into rough chunks (like the courgette)
1 tablespoon olive oil
2 teaspoons baharat, or 1 teaspoon ground cumin and 1 teaspoon paprika
2 tablespoons harissa
Salt and pepper

FOR THE BULGUR WHEAT SALAD
175g (6oz) dry bulgur wheat, or 500g (1lb 2oz) cooked bulgur
Vegetable stock cube, if cooking the bulgur yourself
1 red chilli, finely chopped (deseed if you want less heat)
2 garlic cloves, crushed or finely chopped
Handful of finely chopped dill
Handful of finely chopped mint
Handful of finely chopped parsley
1 teaspoon clear honey
4 tablespoons lemon juice, plus zest of 2 lemons (or reduce the lemon juice and add a splash of red wine vinegar)
2 tablespoons olive oil
Flaked or chopped almonds (optional)

TO SERVE (optional)
450g Greek yogurt
1 teaspoon honey
2 garlic cloves, crushed or finely chopped
Extra olive oil and lemon juice
Fresh dill, chopped

1 Preheat the grill.

2 Combine the olive oil, salt, pepper, baharat and harissa, then divide equally between two bowls. Toss the broccoli and courgette in one bowl, and the paneer in the other.

3 Place the vegetables on a large baking tray and grill for 10 minutes. Give the vegetables a shake and add the paneer. Continue grilling for another 10 minutes, finishing with a couple of minutes at a high heat until lightly charred.

4 If using dry bulgur, rinse it in a sieve. Dissolve the stock cube according to the packet instructions. Place in a pan, add the rinsed bulgur and cook for 10–15 minutes. Drain well. If using pre-cooked bulgur, simply warm through and set aside.

5 While the bulgur wheat cooks and the vegetables and paneer are grilling, combine the red chilli, garlic, dill, mint and parsley in a small bowl.

6 Once the bulgur is cooked and still warm, place in a large bowl and toss with the herb mixture, plus 1 teaspoon honey and most of the lemon zest. Allow the mixture to cool slightly. Add the olive oil and most of the lemon juice along with the flaked almonds, if desired.

7 Add the grilled vegetables and paneer to the bulgur mixture. Toss gently to combine and season to taste.

8 To serve, combine the yogurt with the remaining lemon zest and juice, honey and garlic. Spread this mixture on a large serving platter or individual plates. Place the bulgur, vegetables and paneer on top of the yogurt. Drizzle with a little extra olive oil and lemon juice, if desired.

9 Serve warm or at room temperature with a final sprinkle of dill to finish.

SERVES: 2 • PREP TIME: 15 MINUTES • COOK TIME: 5 MINUTES

Crispy Noodle Salad with Sweet Chilli Paneer

I spent a few months travelling around Nepal in my twenties, and it's still one of my favourite places. It boasts a rich, generous culture, delicious food and, of course, the Himalayas. I spent some time hiking there and, even with limited supplies at 4,000 metres, one dish was always on the menu: 'wai wai sadheko' – a crispy noodle 'salad' with chilli, lemon, peanuts, onion and ALL the seasoning, often tossed through with egg. I ate plates of it, day after day.

This version is in homage to that very delicious sadheko. You don't need to cook the instant noodles as they're already pre-cooked, giving the dish its satisfyingly crunchy, moreish texture.

120g packet instant noodles (such as Shin Ramyun), crushed while still in the packet
Sachet seasoning from the noodle packet
1 teaspoon neutral oil
200g (7oz) paneer, cut into small cubes
1 tablespoon sweet chilli sauce
2 teaspoons soy sauce
Toasted peanuts, to finish

FOR THE DRESSING
2 tablespoons lime juice
1 tablespoon olive oil
½ teaspoon chilli oil (optional)

FOR THE SADHEKO SALAD BASE
1 small red onion, very finely chopped
1 green chilli, finely chopped (deseed if you want less heat)
1 tomato, finely diced
1 cucumber, finely diced
3 spring onions, finely sliced
1 large handful of coriander, finely chopped

1 Tip the crushed noodles into a bowl, reserving a spoonful for garnish, and toss with ¾ teaspoon seasoning from the sachet, reserving the remainder. Set aside. (No cooking is needed.)

2 Prepare the glaze for the paneer by heating the oil in a heavy-based frying pan over a medium–high heat. Fry the paneer until golden on all sides.

3 Lower the heat and add the sweet chilli sauce and soy sauce. Toss for 2–3 minutes, until sticky and caramelized. Watch closely as the sweet chilli can burn. Remove the pan from the heat.

4 To make the dressing, whisk together the remaining sachet seasoning (to taste, as some can be very spicy!) with the lime juice, olive oil and chilli oil, if using.

5 In a large bowl, make the salad base by combining the seasoned noodles, onion, chilli, tomato, cucumber, spring onions and fresh coriander.

6 Add the warm paneer and toss gently. Spoon over the dressing and toss again.

7 Serve immediately to preserve the noodles' crispness, garnished with the toasted peanuts and reserved crushed noodles.

SERVES: 2 AS A MAIN, 4 AS A STARTER • PREP TIME: 10 MINUTES • COOK TIME: 15 MINUTES

Sun-dried Tomato, Olive & Orzo Salad

Sun-dried tomatoes and olives live permanently in my pantry and both offer easy ways to pack flavour into a salad. Paired with garlic and herb paneer, the combination works so well it's silly.

500g (1lb 2oz) cooked orzo or giant couscous, or 125g (4½oz) dry orzo or couscous
Olive oil, for drizzling and frying
200g (7oz) All the Aunties Garlic & Herb Paneer, cut into 2.5-cm (1-inch) cubes
100g (3½oz) sun-dried tomatoes, finely chopped
3 tablespoons olives (such as Kalamata), finely chopped, or 1 tablespoon tapenade
½ red onion, thinly diced
2 large handfuls of spinach, chopped if mature
Pinch of sumac or squeeze of lemon (the zest is lovely here too)
1–2 tablespoons pesto
Salt

1. If using dry orzo or couscous, cook according to the packet instructions. Dry orzo will need 8–10 minutes until al dente, at which point, drain it and add a drizzle of olive oil to prevent sticking. Set aside to cool.
2. Heat 1–2 tablespoons olive oil in a heavy-based frying pan over a medium heat. Fry the paneer cubes for 6–8 minutes, turning occasionally, until golden on all sides and slightly crisp at the edges. Set aside.
3. In a large bowl, combine the sun-dried tomatoes, olives, red onion, spinach, 2 tablespoons olive oil, the sumac or lemon juice and the pesto. Gently rub the spinach leaves between your hands to soften them slightly. Taste and adjust the seasoning with salt and pesto.
4. Toss the garlic and herb paneer with the salad to combine and serve.

SERVES: 2 • PREP TIME: 15 MINUTES • COOK TIME: 20 MINUTES

Charred Corn & Avocado Salad with Blackened Paneer

Inspired by my Sima Aunty, this salad combines pickled jalapeños, coriander and ground cumin. A version of this always finds its way onto our table at Diwali.

200g (7oz) paneer, cut into 2.5-cm (1-inch) cubes
1 tablespoon olive oil
1 teaspoon smoked paprika
½ teaspoon ground cumin
½ teaspoon ground coriander
¼–½ teaspoon cayenne or Aleppo pepper
Salt and pepper

FOR THE SALAD

4 ears of corn, husks removed, or 2 x 340-g (12-oz) cans of corn kernels, drained
2 teaspoons olive oil
1 green bell pepper, deseeded and diced
1 red bell pepper, deseeded and diced
1 small red onion, finely diced
1 large or 2 small avocados, peeled, stoned and diced
4 tablespoons pickled jalapeños, chopped
150g (5½oz) cherry tomatoes, quartered
1 large handful of fresh coriander, leaves torn

FOR THE DRESSING

1 tablespoon pickled jalapeño juice
1 tablespoon lime juice and zest of ½ lime
1 tablespoon olive oil
1 teaspoon ground cumin
1 teaspoon clear honey (to taste)
1 small garlic clove, crushed or finely chopped (optional)
Crushed nachos

TO SERVE

Crushed nachos
Lime wedges

1 Toss the paneer in a bowl with the olive oil, smoked paprika, cumin, coriander and cayenne, then add salt and pepper.

2 Heat the olive oil in a heavy-based frying pan or griddle pan over a high heat. Cook the paneer for 2–3 minutes each side, until deeply charred and blackened at the edges. (This can be done under a hot grill if you prefer.) Set the paneer aside.

3 Using the same pan, cook the corn over a high heat, turning regularly until charred all over. If you prefer, the corn can be charred under a hot grill.

4 When cool enough to handle, cut the kernels off the cobs.

5 Combine the corn, peppers, red onion, avocado, jalapeños, tomatoes and coriander in a large bowl.

6 Whisk together all the dressing ingredients, then spoon over the salad. Gently fold in the blackened paneer.

7 Top with crushed nachos for texture, before serving with lime wedges.

SERVES: 2–3 • PREP TIME: 15 MINUTES • COOK TIME: 15 MINUTES

Grilled Peach Panzanella with Hot-honey Paneer

This is the very first recipe we posted on the All the Aunties Instagram. Filmed over a full day with a wobbly tripod and plenty of on-camera eating, it was made with huge amounts of love and effort. It remains one of our most popular recipes to this day – and for good reason.

Paneer works brilliantly in place of mozzarella: warm, soft and perfect for soaking up all the juices. Best eaten fresh, ideally with a glass of rosé.

200g (7oz) paneer, cut into chunky cubes

FOR THE SALAD BASE

2 thick slices of stale bread, torn into large chunks
Olive oil, for brushing
4 ripe peaches, quartered
2 large handfuls of rocket or watercress
½ red onion, very finely sliced
Salt and pepper

FOR THE HOT HONEY

1½ tablespoons clear honey
½ teaspoon chilli flakes (to taste)
½ teaspoon vinegar

FOR THE DRESSING

3 tablespoons olive oil
2 tablespoons balsamic vinegar
1 tablespoon honey
2 teaspoons dijon mustard

TO SERVE

2 tablespoons toasted flaked almonds
Small handful of basil leaves
Small handful of mint leaves

1. Preheat the oven to 200°C (400°F), Gas Mark 6. For the salad base, toss the bread chunks with a little olive oil and bake for about 15 minutes, until golden and crisp.
2. In a bowl, mix the hot honey ingredients together.
3. Heat a heavy-based frying pan over a medium heat. Add the peaches cut-side down and cook until lightly charred, about 2 minutes per side. Set aside to cool slightly, then slice each quarter in half.
4. In the same pan, fry the paneer cubes until golden on all sides, adding hot honey in the final minute of cooking to evenly coat the paneer and caramelize.
5. Whisk the dressing ingredients together until smooth.
6. On a large platter or in a serving bowl, combine the toasted bread, grilled peaches, rocket, red onion and hot-honey paneer while still warm. Drizzle with the dressing.
7. Sprinkle over the toasted almonds, basil and mint leaves. Serve immediately.

SERVES: 4 • PREP TIME: 10 MINUTES • COOK TIME: 35 MINUTES

Kung Pao Paneer Salad with Pak Choi & Crispy Rice

A recipe dedicated to me, made up entirely of my favourite things. This salad has it all: kung pao flavours, lots of texture from nuts, crispy rice and sticky paneer with charred pak choi. I'm in heaven.

500g (1lb 2oz) cooked jasmine or basmati rice, cooled (made from about 175g/6oz uncooked rice)
Neutral oil, for drizzling and frying
2 tablespoons soy sauce
400g (14oz) paneer, cut into 2.5-cm (1-inch) cubes
2 pak choi, quartered lengthways
1 cucumber, diced
3 spring onions, finely sliced

FOR THE SAUCE AND DRESSING
4 tablespoons soy sauce
2 tablespoons black rice vinegar or other rice vinegar
2 tablespoons clear honey
1½ tablespoons chilli oil (or to taste)
1½ tablespoons toasted sesame oil
2.5-cm (1-inch) piece of fresh root ginger, finely chopped
2 garlic cloves, crushed or finely chopped
1 teaspoon sugar
2 tablespoons lime juice
1 teaspoon cornflour, for the sauce
1 tablespoon water or light stock

TO SERVE
2 tablespoons crispy onions
2 tablespoons roasted peanuts
Dried red chillies, lightly crushed (optional)
Handful of fresh coriander, chopped
Squeeze of lime juice

1. Preheat the oven to 220°C (425°F), Gas Mark 7. Line a tray with baking paper.
2. Spread the fully cooled rice on the prepared tray. Drizzle with neutral oil and the soy sauce, and toss gently to coat. Bake for 30–40 minutes, turning once halfway through, until the rice is golden and crisp, with the grains remaining separate. Set aside to cool slightly.
3. Mix the sauce ingredients together in a bowl, combining everything up to the lime juice. Set aside.
4. Now mix the cornflour with the water or stock in a bowl until smooth.
5. Heat 1 tablespoon neutral oil in a heavy-based frying pan over a medium–high heat. Add the cubed paneer and fry until golden on all sides. Pour in half the sauce and the cornflour slurry. Cook for 2–3 minutes, tossing, until sticky and caramelized. Remove from the heat.
6. Wipe out the pan, and add 1 teaspoon neutral oil. Heat until hot, then add the pak choi, cut-side down. Sear for 1–2 minutes, until lightly charred but still crisp.
7. If necessary, whisk the remaining sauce with a little lime juice and water to make a pourable dressing (you might be able to skip this step). Adjust the consistency and seasoning as needed.
8. In a large bowl, gently combine the cooled crispy rice, seared pak choi, cucumber and spring onions. Place the warm paneer on top and spoon over enough dressing to coat lightly. Toss gently.
9. Sprinkle with the crispy onions, peanuts, crushed chillies and coriander, adding a squeeze of lime just before serving. Serve immediately.

SERVES: 2 • PREP TIME: 15 MINUTES • COOK TIME: 10 MINUTES

Supergreen Goddess Salad

I'm not usually one for Instagram trends, but the green goddess salad and dressing trend can have my screen time any day. It's everything a salad dressing should be: creamy, salty, tart, umami and, for me, a little spicy. This is my version.

125g (4½oz) kale, stems removed and leaves roughly chopped
1 tablespoon lemon juice
2 tablespoons olive oil, plus extra for frying
Pinch of salt
1 large handful of baby spinach
½ small cucumber, diced
35g (1¼oz) red cabbage, finely shredded
6–8 pink radishes, very thinly sliced (optional)
200g (7oz) All the Aunties Garlic & Herb Paneer, cut into chunky cubes
2 tablespoons Pickled Red Onions (see page 111), to garnish
4 tablespoons toasted pumpkin and sunflower seeds, to garnish

FOR THE DRESSING
1 ripe avocado
1 small garlic clove, crushed or finely chopped
2 tablespoons Greek yogurt
2 tablespoons olive oil
1–2 tablespoons pickled jalapeños, plus 1 teaspoon of their brine
2 anchovies, or 1 teaspoon of miso for a vegetarian alternative (optional)
2 tablespoons lemon juice
Small handful of chopped basil
Small handful of chopped parsley
Small handful of chopped chives or dill
2–4 tablespoons cold water to loosen
Salt and sugar, to taste

1 In a large bowl, combine the kale with the lemon juice, olive oil and a pinch of salt. Massage for 1–2 minutes until the kale softens slightly and turns a deeper green.

2 Add the spinach, cucumber, red cabbage and radishes, if using. Toss gently to combine, adding more olive oil if needed.

3 Heat a little oil in a heavy-based frying pan over a medium heat. Add the paneer cubes and cook until the edges are golden. Let the paneer develop a rich colour before turning.

4 To make the dressing, place the avocado, garlic and yogurt in a blender or food processor, and add the olive oil, jalapeños and brine, the anchovies (if using), lemon juice and herbs. Blend until completely smooth. Gradually add the measured cold water until the dressing reaches a thick but spoonable consistency. Taste and adjust with salt, lemon juice or sugar. (Note that salt may be unnecessary if using anchovies or miso.)

5 Spoon enough dressing over the greens to coat them evenly and toss gently. Top with the warm paneer, pickled red onions and toasted seeds. Serve immediately so the paneer remains warm and the greens stay crisp.

SERVES: 2–3 • PREP TIME: 15 MINUTES • COOK TIME: 30 MINUTES

Warm Preserved Lemon, Apricot & Harissa Salad

Pearl barley is a hearty grain that is excellent at absorbing flavour, while dried fruit is an easy way to add texture and sweetness. Both work beautifully in this salad, inspired by Moroccan tagines.

150g (5½oz) dried pearl barley
1 tablespoon olive oil
200g (7oz) paneer, cut into bite-sized cubes
1 small red onion, thinly sliced
4 teaspoons rose harissa
½ teaspoon ground cumin
½ teaspoon ground coriander
¼ teaspoon ground cinnamon
2 garlic cloves, crushed or finely grated
200g (7oz) Tenderstem broccoli, cut into 4–5-cm (1½–2-inch) lengths
1 preserved lemon, pulp removed and rind finely chopped
6 dried apricots, finely chopped
1–2 teaspoons clear honey
1 tablespoon lemon juice
Salt

FOR THE DRESSING
150g (5½oz) thick Greek yogurt
2 teaspoons rose harissa
1 teaspoon clear honey
1 tablespoon lemon juice

FOR THE GREMOLATA
30g (1oz) pine nuts, roughly chopped and lightly toasted
Zest of ½ lemon
Small handful of flat-leaf parsley or coriander, finely chopped
1 tablespoon olive oil

1. Cook the pearl barley in well-salted water until tender but still with a bit of bite (20–25 minutes). Drain well and set aside.
2. Heat half the olive oil in a wide, heavy-based frying pan and fry the paneer until golden all over. Remove and set aside.
3. Add the remaining oil to the pan and cook the onion gently until softened.
4. Stir in the harissa, cumin, coriander, cinnamon and garlic. Cook for 30 seconds until fragrant.
5. Add the broccoli and cook for 3–4 minutes, until just tender.
6. Return the paneer to the pan, then add the barley, preserved lemon rind, apricots and honey. Toss gently to combine.
7. Take off the heat, squeeze over the lemon juice and season to taste.
8. Mix the dressing ingredients together with a pinch of salt until smooth.
9. To make the gremolata, combine the pine nuts with the lemon zest, chopped herbs, olive oil and salt.
10. Spoon the warm barley mixture into bowls. Drizzle generously with the dressing, then sprinkle over the gremolata.

CURRIES & COMPANY

SERVES: 4 • PREP TIME: 25 MINUTES • COOK TIME: 60–90 MINUTES

Red Kidney Bean & Paneer Curry

Also known as rajma, this is a traditional Punjabi dish that my mum would make on a weekend, in a big bowl with lots of rotlis. The next day we'd have it with crushed tortilla chips over the top and some 'salsa' and guacamole on the side. The key to a good rajma is to take your time with each step: allow the onions to turn golden, and the tomatoes to caramelize and develop flavour.

250g (9oz) dried rajma (red kidney beans), soaked overnight, or 2 x 400-g (14-oz) cans, drained
Salt

FOR THE CURRY
2 tablespoons oil or ghee
1 bay leaf
1 black cardamom pod (optional but authentic)
4 green cardamom pods
3 cloves
1 teaspoon cumin seeds
1 large red onion, very finely chopped
2 tablespoons ginger-garlic paste
2 green chillies, slit lengthways (deseed if you want less heat)
3 large tomatoes, finely chopped or puréed
1 tablespoon tomato purée (optional)
1 teaspoon Kashmiri (mild) chilli powder
1½ teaspoons ground coriander
1 teaspoon ground cumin
½ teaspoon ground turmeric
1–2 teaspoons garam masala
1 tablespoon kasoori methi, crushed
200g (7oz) paneer, cut into small cubes

TO FINISH
Fresh coriander, roughly chopped
Squeeze of lemon juice

1. If using dried rajma, drain the soaked beans and pressure-cook with salt until very soft. They should mash easily between your fingers. Reserve some cooking liquid. Alternatively, simmer the drained beans in a large pan of salted water for 60–90 minutes, or until very soft, topping up with water as needed. Reserve some of the cooking liquid.

2. Heat the oil or ghee in a heavy-based frying pan. Add the bay leaf, cardamom pods, cloves and cumin seeds and cook for 30–60 seconds, until fragrant.

3. Add the onion and cook slowly until deeply golden, about 10–12 minutes. This stage builds flavour.

4. Add the ginger-garlic paste and green chillies. Cook for 1 minute.

5. Add the tomatoes and tomato purée, if using. Cook down for about 8–10 minutes until thick, glossy and the oil begins to separate.

6. Add the chilli powder, coriander, cumin and turmeric. Cook for 30 seconds, stirring constantly.

7. Add the cooked rajma along with some of the cooking liquid (or hot water if using canned beans). Simmer gently for 20–30 minutes. Stir occasionally and mash a few beans against the side of the pan to thicken the gravy naturally. The consistency should be creamy and slightly thick – not watery.

8. Add the garam masala and crushed kasoori methi. Gently fold in the paneer cubes and simmer for 3–4 minutes, just until warmed through.

9. Finish with fresh coriander and lemon. Allow the curry to rest for 10 minutes before serving.

SERVES: 4 • PREP TIME: 25 MINUTES • COOK TIME: 40 MINUTES

Dill & Fennel Dal with Asparagus

In the western world, dal is often thought of as a dish for winter. But we eat it all year round, and it changes with the seasons. This recipe is inspired by my mum's legendary dill dal, and is light and joyful - perfect for spring. Like diving into a bowl of daffodils.

300g (10 ½ oz) moong (split yellow lentils)
800ml–1 litre (1¾ pints) stock or water
1 teaspoon ground turmeric
1 teaspoon ground cumin
2 teaspoons salt
2 tablespoons ghee
1 teaspoon fennel seeds
1 teaspoon cumin seeds
1 leek, finely sliced
1 fennel bulb, finely sliced (reserve the fronds if fresh)
2.5-cm (1-inch) piece of fresh root ginger, finely grated
6 garlic cloves, grated
1 red chilli, finely diced (deseed if you want less heat)
175g (6oz) asparagus tips, chopped
200g (7oz) paneer, cut into small cubes or roughly crumbled
Zest and juice of 1 lemon
4 spring onions, finely chopped
1 handful of fresh dill, finely chopped (6–7 fronds)

Customize your dal to taste using warming spices, such as cinnamon, chilli and cloves for a cold day, and fennel, ginger and lemon for a warmer one. You can't really go wrong.

1. Rinse the split yellow lentils thoroughly under a cold tap until the water runs mostly clear.
2. Place the lentils in a large saucepan with the stock or water. Bring to the boil, skim off any foam, then reduce to a simmer. Add the turmeric and cumin, plus 1 teaspoon of the salt. Cook for 30–40 minutes, until the lentils are completely soft and beginning to break down. Stir occasionally and add more hot water if needed – the texture should be loose and spoonable, not thick like mash. If it is too thick, add more water.
3. While the lentils cook, heat the ghee in a wide pan over a medium heat. Add the fennel seeds and cumin seeds and let them sizzle until fragrant.
4. Add the sliced leek and fennel to the pan with a pinch of salt. Cook gently for about 10 minutes, until soft and slightly sweet but not browned.
5. Add the ginger and garlic to the pan, along with the red chilli. Cook for 1–2 minutes, until fragrant. Stir in the asparagus tips and cook for 2–3 minutes so they stay bright and slightly crisp.
6. Once the lentils are soft, stir in the cooked leek and fennel mixture. Add a little hot water if needed to loosen – this dal should be silky and flowing.
7. Fold in the paneer and simmer gently for 3–4 minutes to warm through. Don't overcook or the paneer will firm up.
8. Add the remaining teaspoon of salt (or to taste), the lemon zest and most of the juice. Stir in the spring onions and a generous handful of dill.
9. Taste and adjust with more lemon juice if needed. The dal should be lemony and fresh.

SERVES: 4 • PREP TIME: 15–20 MINUTES • COOK TIME: 25–30 MINUTES

Matar Paneer

When I tell people I run a paneer business, I'm often met with, 'Oh, I *love* Matar Paneer'. And who can blame them? It's a classic: simple, comforting and always a crowd-pleaser.

2 tablespoons oil or ghee
1 tablespoon butter
1 teaspoon cumin seeds
1–2 bay leaves
1 cinnamon stick
4 green cardamom pods, lightly crushed
4 cloves
2 onions, finely chopped
2 tablespoons ginger-garlic paste
2 green chillies, finely chopped
1 tablespoon tomato purée
3 large ripe tomatoes, finely chopped, or 400-g (14-oz) can chopped tomatoes
1½ teaspoons ground coriander
1 teaspoon Kashmiri (mild) chilli powder
½ teaspoon ground turmeric
1 teaspoon ground cumin
Sugar, to taste
300g (10½oz) frozen green peas
400g (14oz) paneer, cut into 2.5-cm (1-inch) cubes
2–3 tablespoons single cream
1 tablespoon kasoori methi, crushed
Salt, to taste

TO FINISH
1 teaspoon garam masala
Fresh coriander, roughly chopped

1. Heat the oil and butter in a heavy-based frying pan. Add the cumin seeds, bay leaves, cinnamon stick, cardamom pods and cloves. Let them sizzle gently until fragrant.
2. Add the onions and cook them slowly for 8–10 minutes, until soft and golden. Add the ginger-garlic paste and the green chillies. Cook for 1 minute.
3. Add the tomato purée and cook for a few minutes to remove any metallic flavour.
4. Blitz the tomatoes in a blender or food processor until smooth. Add to the pan. Cook for about 5 minutes, until thick, glossy and slightly reduced, so the oil begins to separate at the edges and it thickens into a paste.
5. Stir in the ground coriander, chilli powder, turmeric, cumin, sugar and salt and cook for 1 minute. Loosen with 100–150ml (3½–5fl oz) water and add the peas. Simmer for 8–10 minutes until the peas are tender and the gravy thickens.
6. Add the paneer to the pan and simmer gently for just 3–4 minutes.
7. Stir in the cream, then add the kasoori methi.
8. Sprinkle with the garam masala and chopped coriander before serving.

This is a brilliantly easy dish for the Instant Pot. Add all the ingredients and let them cook down, then stir in the paneer and peas for the final five minutes.

SERVES: 4 • PREP TIME: 20–25 MINUTES • COOK TIME: 25–30 MINUTES

Paneer Butter Masala with Brown Butter Tadka

This is our take on a classic, with a generous amount of whole spices and blended walnuts in the base. The tadka mirrors the nuttiness in the dish and is well worth the extra few minutes.

1 tablespoon ghee or neutral oil
6 green cardamom pods
5 cloves
5-cm (2-inch) cinnamon stick
2 bay leaves
2 teaspoons cumin seeds
2 onions, finely chopped
3 tablespoons ginger-garlic paste
2 green chillies, slit lengthways, (deseed if you want less heat)
1 teaspoon Kashmiri (mild) chilli powder
1 teaspoon ground turmeric
1 tablespoon tomato purée
400g (14oz) paneer, cut into 2.5-cm (1-inch) cubes
1 tablespoon kasoori methi
1 tablespoon cashew cream, or single cream
1½ teaspoons garam masala
1–2 teaspoons clear honey
Salt, to taste

FOR THE NUT MIXTURE
2 fresh tomatoes (add a pinch of sugar if out of season)
70g (2½oz) cashews or 50–55g (1¾–2oz) walnuts, soaked in water for 30 minutes

FOR THE BROWN BUTTER TADKA
1 tablespoon butter
2.5-cm (1-inch) piece of fresh root ginger, sliced
2 garlic cloves, finely sliced
Pinch of chilli powder
Pinch of cumin seeds

1. Heat the oil or ghee in a pan over a medium heat. Add the cardamom pods, cloves, cinnamon stick, bay leaves and cumin seeds. Sauté until fragrant, stirring constantly to prevent burning.
2. Add the onions and a pinch of salt. Cook for 5–10 minutes, until golden brown, stirring frequently.
3. Meanwhile, make the nut and tomato mixture: place the tomatoes, soaked nuts and 1 tablespoon of their soaking liquid in a blender or food processor. Blitz until smooth, adding a splash of water if the mixture is too thick.
4. Add the ginger-garlic paste and green chillies to the onions. Cook for 2 minutes, stirring continuously.
5. Stir in the chilli powder and turmeric. Cook for 1 minute.
6. Add the tomato purée and cook for another minute, then stir in the blended nut and tomato mixture. Simmer for 15 minutes, until the mixture thickens and begins to pull away from the sides of the pan. Gradually add water to loosen, but keep the sauce thick.
7. Gently stir in the paneer and kasoori methi. Simmer for 2–3 minutes, until the paneer is heated through.
8. Stir in the cashew cream (it works beautifully here), garam masala and honey.
9. For the brown butter tadka, melt the butter in a small pan and place over a medium heat until golden brown. Add the ginger, garlic, chilli powder and cumin seeds. Cook for 30–60 seconds, until aromatic, then pour over the curry and serve immediately.

Make sure your mixture is thick and fragrant before you start rehydrating with water. This is key for developing good flavour.

SERVES: 4 • PREP TIME: 20 MINUTES • COOK TIME: 30 MINUTES

Supergreen Saag Paneer

This is our family version of another classic. We like to make it supergreen – a combination of spinach, kale and whatever is in season. Cook it just enough to retain the colour and freshness. It's bright, nourishing and full of flavour.

Neutral oil, for frying
400g (14oz) paneer, cut into 2.5-cm (1-inch) cubes
200g (7oz) baby spinach leaves
50g (1¾oz) kale, tough stems removed
125g (4½oz) spring greens, tough stems removed
1 tablespoon ghee or neutral oil
2 onions, diced
2–3 green chillies, slit lengthways (deseed if you want less heat)
6 garlic cloves, crushed or finely chopped
5-cm (2-inch) piece of fresh root ginger, finely sliced
1 ripe tomato, sliced
60g (2¼oz) yogurt
¼ teaspoon ground turmeric
2 teaspoons ground cumin
2 teaspoons ground coriander
½ teaspoon chilli powder
1 teaspoon salt
½ teaspoon sugar
150–200ml (5–7fl oz) water
1 teaspoon garam masala

TO SERVE
2–3 tablespoons cashew cream
1 tablespoon kasoori methi (dried fenugreek leaves), crushed
Fresh coriander (optional)
1 quantity garlic-ginger tadka (see page 162; optional)

1. Heat a tablespoon of oil in a frying pan and fry the paneer cubes for 3–4 minutes until lightly golden. Set aside.
2. Wash the spinach, kale and spring greens well and let them drain. Don't worry about the amount – they will shrink significantly when cooked.
3. Heat the ghee or oil in a pan over a medium heat. Add the onions, green chillies, garlic and ginger. Cook for 6–8 minutes, until the onions are soft and lightly golden.
4. Add the tomato and cook until softened and slightly jammy.
5. Add the greens and cook until completely wilted.
6. Transfer this mixture to a blender or food processor. Add the yogurt, turmeric, cumin, coriander, chilli powder, salt, sugar and measured water, then blitz until smooth or slightly coarse, depending on your preferred texture. Return the mixture to the pan.
7. Let the saag simmer gently. Stir in the garam masala, then add the fried paneer and warm through for 2–3 minutes.
8. Finish with a drizzle of cashew cream and a sprinkle of kasoori methi. Garnish either with fresh coriander or a garlic-ginger tadka, if using, before serving.

SERVES: 4 • PREP TIME: 25 MINUTES • COOK TIME: 25 MINUTES

Green Curry with Lime Leaf Paneer

Thai green curry dialled up a notch. A few extra vegetables and some proper aromatics take a shop-bought paste from good to genuinely great.

1 stick of lemongrass, finely minced
3 makrut lime leaves, stems discarded then very finely shredded
2 garlic cloves, crushed or grated
Zest and juice of 1 lime
4 teaspoons soy sauce
1 teaspoon soft brown sugar
1 teaspoon neutral oil
400g (14oz) paneer, cut into cubes and scored

FOR THE GREEN CURRY
1 tablespoon neutral oil
2–2½ tablespoons Thai green curry paste (or to taste)
2.5-cm (1-inch) piece of fresh root ginger, finely chopped
2 large handfuls of spinach
400ml (14fl oz) full-fat coconut milk
100ml (3½fl oz) vegetable stock (if needed for desired consistency)
1 tablespoon peanut butter or tahini
2 teaspoons soy sauce
2 teaspoons (vegan) fish sauce
2 teaspoons soft brown sugar
Small handful of fresh coriander
150g (5oz) Tenderstem broccoli, cut into 5-cm (2-inch) lengths
100g (3½oz) green beans
1 tablespoon lime juice
Small handful of Thai basil leaves

TO SERVE
Steamed jasmine rice
Fresh coriander, chopped
Lime wedges

1. In a bowl, mix the lemongrass, lime leaves, garlic, lime juice and zest, soy sauce, sugar and oil. Add the paneer and toss gently to coat. Leave to marinate for at least 15 minutes (or up to an hour for more flavour).

2. Heat a griddle or frying pan over a medium–high heat. Cook the paneer for 2–3 minutes per side, without overcrowding, until golden and lightly charred. Set aside.

3. To make the green curry, heat the oil in a wide pan. Add the green curry paste and cook for 1–2 minutes, stirring, until fragrant.

4. Using a blender or food processor, blitz the ginger, spinach, coconut milk, peanut butter or tahini, soy sauce, fish sauce, sugar and coriander until smooth.

5. Pour the blended curry into the pan with the paste and simmer gently for about 15 minutes, stirring occasionally and adding the vegetable stock if needed to loosen.

6. Add the broccoli and green beans. Cook for 4–5 minutes, until tender but still bright in colour.

7. Stir in the lime juice, then add the cooked paneer to warm through.

8. Remove from the heat and fold in the Thai basil. Serve immediately with jasmine rice, fresh coriander and lime wedges.

SERVES: 4 • PREP TIME: 20 MINUTES • COOK TIME: 20 MINUTES

Keralan-inspired Beetroot & Coconut Curry

Beetroot is the star here: its earthiness and gorgeous pink colour are irresistible, even for those who aren't usually fans.

1 onion, sliced
6 garlic cloves, crushed or finely chopped
3.5-cm (1½-inch) piece of fresh root ginger, finely chopped
3 teaspoons ground cumin
2 teaspoons ground coriander
1 teaspoon ground black pepper
1 teaspoon chilli powder
½ teaspoon ground turmeric
2 tablespoons coconut oil
4 green cardamom pods
4 cloves
1 cinnamon stick
350–400g (12–14oz) cooked beetroot, roughly chopped
200ml (7fl oz) vegetable stock
400ml (14fl oz) coconut milk
Pinch of sugar
Salt, to taste

FOR THE MANGO-GLAZED PANEER
400g (14oz) paneer, cut into 2.5-cm (1-inch) cubes
2 tablespoons Mango Chutney (see page 169)

FOR THE TADKA
1 tablespoon ghee or butter
1 teaspoon fennel seeds
1 teaspoon mustard seeds
10–12 fresh curry leaves
1 green chilli, finely sliced (deseed if you want less heat)

TO SERVE
Fresh coriander
Crispy onions (optional)

1. Using a blender or food processor, blitz the onion, garlic, ginger and ground spices into a thick paste. Add a splash of water if needed to blend smoothly.
2. Heat the coconut oil in a heavy-based pan over a medium heat. Add the cardamom pods, cloves and cinnamon stick and fry for 30–40 seconds, until fragrant.
3. Add the blended paste and cook for 2–3 minutes, stirring, until it darkens slightly and is fragrant.
4. In the same blender or food processor, blitz the beetroot with the stock and coconut milk until smooth, then pour into the pan.
5. Bring to a gentle simmer and cook for 15–20 minutes, until slightly thickened. Add a pinch of sugar and season to taste with salt.
6. While the curry simmers, fry the paneer in a separate pan until golden on all sides. Add the mango chutney and cook for 1–2 minutes, turning the paneer so it becomes lightly glazed and sticky.
7. To make the tadka, heat the ghee or butter in a small pan. Add the seeds and fry until they begin to pop. Add the curry leaves and chilli and cook for a few seconds more until fragrant.
8. Serve the curry topped with the mango-glazed paneer, the hot tadka, fresh coriander and crispy onions, if you wish.

SERVES: 2 • PREP TIME: 15 MINUTES • COOK TIME: 20 MINUTES

Paneer Katsu Curry

I made this during lockdown for my mum. She was initially sceptical – largely, I suspect, because of the 'curry powder', which borders on blasphemous in our household – but over time her love for this dish has grown. This is an easy at-home version that has been refined over time. The paneer is perfect for scooping up the rich sauce.

100g (3½oz) panko breadcrumbs
1–2 tablespoons black and white sesame seeds
1 egg, beaten
2 tablespoons plain flour
½ teaspoon mild curry powder
200g (7oz) paneer, torn into 2.5-cm (1-inch) chunks
Neutral oil, for shallow-frying
Salt and pepper

FOR THE SAUCE
1 tablespoon neutral oil
1 onion, finely chopped
1 carrot, finely chopped or grated
4 garlic cloves, crushed or grated
2.5-cm (1-inch) piece of fresh root ginger, finely chopped or grated
¼ teaspoon ground turmeric
1 tablespoon mild curry powder
1 tablespoon plain flour
600ml (20fl oz) chicken or vegetable stock
1 tablespoon soy sauce
1 teaspoon clear honey (optional)

TO SERVE
Steamed rice
Spring onions or sesame seeds

1 First make the sauce: heat the oil in a heavy-based saucepan over a medium heat. Add the onion and carrot and cook for 5–6 minutes, until soft. Add the garlic and ginger and cook for 30 seconds.

2 Stir in the turmeric, curry powder and flour and cook for 1 minute. Slowly pour in the stock, stirring constantly to keep the sauce smooth. Add the soy sauce and honey. For a smoother sauce, remove the pan from the heat and blitz with a stick blender, then return to the heat. Simmer for 8–10 minutes, until the sauce thickens enough to coat the back of a spoon. Keep warm.

3 In a bowl, combine the panko breadcrumbs and sesame seeds. Put the beaten egg in a second bowl.

4 In a third bowl, season the flour well with salt, pepper and the curry powder. Coat each piece of paneer in the flour, dip into the beaten egg, then press firmly into the breadcrumb mixture.

5 Heat a shallow layer of oil in a frying pan over a medium heat. Fry the paneer for 2–3 minutes per side, until golden and crisp. Drain briefly on kitchen paper.

6 Serve with bowls of steamed rice, placing the paneer to one side and spooning the curry sauce around it (not over the top, so the paneer stays crisp).

SERVES: 4 • PREP TIME: 15 MINUTES • COOK TIME: 40 MINUTES

Curried Golden Coconut, Carrot & Paneer Soup

A one-pot golden wonder. The cumin and ginger will warm you through on the chilliest of days, and swapping croutons for spiced paneer makes this feel like a proper meal: comforting, filling and full of texture.

400g (14oz) paneer, cut into 2.5-cm (1-inch) cubes
2 tablespoons neutral oil, for frying
1 tablespoon coconut oil
1 medium onion, sliced
4 garlic cloves, crushed or roughly chopped
2.5-cm (1-inch) piece of fresh root ginger, grated
1 red chilli, chopped (deseed if you want less heat) or 1 teaspoon crushed red chilli flakes (optional)
1½ teaspoons ground turmeric
1½ teaspoons ground cumin
4 carrots, roughly chopped
1 sweet potato, finely diced
400ml (14fl oz) full-fat coconut milk
250ml (9fl oz) hot water or vegetable stock
Sugar, to taste
2 tablespoons lime juice
Fine salt
Warm bread, to serve

FOR THE GREENS AND GARNISH
2 large handfuls of cavolo nero or kale, stems discarded, then finely chopped
1 quantity Curry Leaf and Mustard Seed Tadka (optional; see page 162)

1 Heat the neutral oil in a heavy-based pan over a medium heat. Add the paneer cubes and fry for 4–6 minutes, turning gently, until golden on at least two sides. Remove from the pan and set aside.

2 In the same pan, heat the coconut oil. Add the onion with a pinch of salt and cook over a medium heat until completely soft and translucent, about 6–8 minutes, taking care not to brown.

3 Stir in the garlic, ginger and chilli, if using, and cook for about a minute until fragrant. Add the turmeric and cumin and stir gently for 30 seconds to toast the spices without letting them darken.

4 Add the carrots and sweet potato, stirring to coat them thoroughly in the spiced oil. Pour in the coconut milk and hot water, season with salt, and bring to a gentle simmer. Cover and cook for 15–18 minutes, or until the vegetables are completely tender.

5 Remove the pan from the heat and use a blender or food processor to blitz the mixture until completely smooth.

6 Return the smooth soup base to the pan and bring back to a gentle simmer. Add the fried paneer and cook for 3–4 minutes so it warms through and absorbs some flavour. Taste and adjust with additional salt if needed, a teaspoon of sugar if the turmeric feels slightly sharp and the lime juice for brightness.

7 Finally, stir in the cavolo nero (chickpeas would be a good addition here too) and cook for 2–3 minutes, until just tender but still vibrant green.

8 Pour over the tadka, if using. Serve hot with warm bread.

SERVES: 2 AS A MAIN, 4 AS A SIDE • PREP TIME: 15 MINUTES • COOK TIME: 55 MINUTES

Tadka Dal with Confit Garlic

This is my mother's signature dal and, for me, a true taste of home. Using two different lentils – red split and yellow split – gives a superior texture and depth of flavour, elevating what people might normally assume to be simple, everyday cooking. This dish shows that dal can be decadent, rich and delicious. It is a labour of love, but well worth it.

100g (3½ oz) red split lentils
100g (3½ oz) yellow split lentils
475ml (17fl oz) water
1 teaspoon ground turmeric
1–2 teaspoons salt
1 large garlic bulb
1 onion, halved
2–3 tomatoes, halved
Olive oil, for drizzling
1 green chilli, finely chopped (deseed if you want less heat)
½ teaspoon red chilli powder
400g (14oz) paneer, cut into small cubes
Handful of fresh coriander, chopped
1 tablespoon lime juice
Steamed basmati rice or warm flatbreads, to serve

FOR THE TADKA
1 tablespoon oil or ghee
1 bay leaf
2 black or green cardamom pods
4 crushed peppercorns (or plenty of freshly cracked black pepper)
1 teaspoon cumin seeds
¼ teaspoon asafoetida (optional)
1 teaspoon ground cumin
1 teaspoon ground coriander

1 Rinse the red and yellow lentils under a cold tap until the water runs clear. If you wish, you can then soak them for 15–30 minutes (to reduce the cooking time). Drain and transfer to a large pan, then add the water, turmeric and salt. Bring to a gentle boil, then simmer for 20–25 minutes, stirring occasionally, until the lentils are soft but still holding their shape.

2 While the lentils cook, preheat the oven to 180°C (350°F), Gas Mark 4. Cut the stem off the garlic, then wrap the bulb in foil. Place it on a baking tray with the onion and tomatoes. Drizzle with a little oil and roast for 30–40 minutes, turning occasionally, until soft, lightly caramelized and jammy. Remove the garlic skins, then transfer to a blender or food processor along with the green chilli and chilli powder, and blitz until smooth. Taste and adjust seasoning if necessary. Set aside.

3 Now assemble your tadka. In a small pan, warm the oil or ghee over a medium heat. Add the bay leaf, cardamom pods, crushed peppercorns, cumin seeds and asafoetida, if using. Stir gently for 30–60 seconds, until aromatic. Remove from the heat and stir in the cumin and coriander. This ensures the spices release their fragrance without burning.

4 Add the blitzed tomato mixture and cubed paneer to the cooked lentils. Stir gently to combine. Pour in the tadka and mix again, allowing the flavours to infuse. Simmer gently for 5–7 minutes so the paneer warms through and absorbs some of the dal's flavour.

5 Turn off the heat. Stir in the freshly chopped coriander and lime juice. Adjust the salt or chilli if needed.

6 Spoon into bowls and serve immediately with steamed basmati rice or warm flatbreads.

SERVES: 3–4 AS A SIDE • PREP TIME: 10 MINUTES • COOK TIME: 20 MINUTES

Everyday Pilau

Don't get me wrong – there's little better than a bowl of plain white rice with salted butter mixed through. But every now and then, it can be elevated to a full meal with pan-fried paneer, a handful of peas and just five minutes' work. It pairs well with almost everything.

175g (6oz) basmati rice
2 tablespoons ghee or oil
1 teaspoon cumin seeds
1 small potato, cut into small cubes
200g (7oz) paneer, cut into small cubes
70g (2½oz) peas, fresh or frozen
½ teaspoon ground turmeric
½ teaspoon sugar
1 teaspoon salt, or to taste
250ml (9fl oz) hot water
1 tablespoon fresh coriander, chopped (optional)

1. Wash the rice under a cold tap until the water runs clear, then, if you wish, soak for 15–20 minutes. Drain and set aside.
2. Heat the ghee or oil in a saucepan over a medium heat. Add the cumin seeds and let them crackle. Add the diced potato and paneer and cook for 2–3 minutes, until the paneer is slightly golden and the potato begins to soften. Stir in the peas, turmeric, sugar and salt.
3. Add the drained rice to the pan and stir gently for about a minute until the rice is lightly coated in the ghee and spices. Pour in the hot water and bring to the boil. Once boiling, reduce the heat to low, cover with a lid and cook for 10–12 minutes, until the water is absorbed and the rice is tender.
4. Turn off the heat and let it rest, covered, for 5 minutes. Fluff gently with a fork and sprinkle with chopped coriander, if using.
5. Serve alongside dal or mild curries (see image on page 71).

For extra flavour, add a finely diced onion, 2 chopped green chillies and 4 chopped garlic cloves at the same point as the potatoes.

SERVES: 4 (MAKES 8–10 ROTLIS) • PREP TIME: 35 MINUTES • COOK TIME: 15 MINUTES

Rotlis

My family is from Gujarat, so in our house it's not rotis – it's rotlis. I grew up eating these very soft, thin, round flatbreads every day, often hot off the pan with a simple spread of butter and honey.

Among the Aunties it's always a competition to see who makes the best rotli – and in my opinion my grandma, Kusum Baa, was unbeatable. Her rotlis were fast, precise and always perfectly round (unlike mine...I'm still working on it). It is a true skill, and years of experience will give you a softer dough and thinner, rounder rotli – so it's wise to start now!

250g (9oz) wholemeal flour
1 tablespoon neutral oil
120–150ml lukewarm water, plus extra as needed
Butter or ghee, to serve (optional)

1. Place the flour in a wide bowl. Add the oil and rub it in with your fingertips until evenly distributed. Gradually add the lukewarm water, a little at a time, bringing the mixture together into a soft, pliable dough. It should feel smooth and supple, not stiff or dry. Add a little more water if needed, but avoid making it sticky.

2. Knead the dough thoroughly for 8–10 minutes until smooth and elastic. Proper kneading helps develop gluten, which makes the rotli soft and pliable. Cover the dough with a damp cloth and let it rest for at least 20 minutes.

3. Divide the dough into golf ball-sized portions and keep them covered. Lightly dust a portion with flour and roll it into a thin, even circle about 15cm (6 inches) in diameter. The edges should be the same thickness as the centre. Repeat with the remaining dough.

4. Heat a heavy-based frying pan over a medium heat. Place a rolled rotli in the pan. When the underside turns opaque and small bubbles begin to appear, flip it over. Cook the second side until light brown spots form. Flip once more if needed to ensure both sides are lightly cooked.

5. Using tongs, place the rotli directly over a low open flame or onto a wire mesh. It should puff up fully within a few seconds. Remove immediately once ballooned.

6. Brush lightly with butter or ghee, if desired. Keep the rotli covered in a cloth-lined container to maintain softness until serving. Cook the remaining rotlis in the same way, then serve with your favourite curries or paneer dishes.

UNCLE-APPROVED CARBS

SERVES: 4 (MAKES 8–10 CHILLAS) • PREP TIME: 10 MINUTES • COOK TIME: 15 MINUTES

Paneer Chillas

Every Indian household has its own version of these chickpea pancakes – they are endlessly adaptable and almost impossible to get wrong. Throw in whatever vegetables you have, add some spices and you're done. Quick, nutritious and a proper pantry staple.

250g (9oz) chickpea flour
1 teaspoon baking powder
2 teaspoons salt
1 teaspoon carom seeds (ajwain), or a pinch of oregano or thyme
1 teaspoon chilli powder (or to taste)
1 teaspoon ground cumin
1 teaspoon ground coriander
¼ teaspoon asafoetida (or substitute with 1 clove of grated garlic)
¼ teaspoon ground turmeric
1 carrot, finely grated
1 shallot or ½ onion, grated or very finely chopped
½ head of broccoli, grated or very finely chopped
200g (7oz) paneer, grated
1–2 tablespoons fresh coriander, finely chopped
225ml (8fl oz) buttermilk or milk
125–225ml (4–8fl oz) water
Neutral oil, for frying and drizzling

TO SERVE
Coriander Chutney, Tamarind Chutney and Any Veg Pickle (see pages 168 and 170)
Yogurt and a squeeze of lemon

1. In a large mixing bowl, whisk together the chickpea flour, baking powder, salt, carom seeds, chilli powder, cumin, ground coriander, asafoetida and turmeric until evenly combined.
2. Add the carrot, shallot or onion, broccoli, paneer and fresh coriander. Mix well so all the vegetables are coated in the flour mixture.
3. Pour in the buttermilk and begin mixing. Gradually add the water (you might not need all of it), stirring continuously, until you have a smooth batter. You're looking for a pourable consistency that is thinner than pancake batter, but thick enough to coat the back of a spoon. It should also spread easily in the pan.
4. Let the batter rest for 10–15 minutes to thicken slightly. After resting, check the consistency again and loosen with a small splash of water, if needed.
5. Heat a nonstick or well-seasoned pan over a medium heat and lightly brush or drizzle with a little neutral oil. Stir the batter, as the vegetables will have settled slightly, then pour about 50ml (2fl oz) into the centre of the pan. Using the back of a ladle, gently spread it outwards in a circular motion to form a very thin pancake, roughly 3mm thick.
6. Cook for 2–3 minutes, until the surface looks mostly set and the edges begin to dry and lift. Drizzle a little oil around the edges, then flip the pancake carefully and cook for another 2–3 minutes, until golden with lightly crisp edges. Adjust the heat if necessary so the centre cooks through without the outside browning too quickly. Transfer the cooked pancake to a plate and set aside while you cook the rest, oiling the pan each time.
7. Serve the pancakes warm with the chutneys and pickle, or simply yogurt with a squeeze of lemon. They are also excellent folded and packed into lunchboxes.

If you don't have asafoetida, replace it with ½ a finely sliced onion and 1 clove of grated garlic.

SERVES: 4 • PREP TIME: 5 MINUTES • COOK TIME: 5 MINUTES

Sticky Paneer Fried Rice

This simple fried rice delivers every time. Paneer replaces the usual egg, making it a great option for egg-free vegetarians while still being packed with protein. Quick, satisfying and perfect for using up whatever is in the fridge.

2 tablespoons ghee or vegetable oil
6 garlic cloves, crushed or finely chopped
5-cm (2-inch) piece of fresh root ginger, finely chopped
4 spring onions, white parts only, sliced
70g (2oz) frozen peas
1 small carrot, finely diced
200g (7oz) paneer, crumbled
1 teaspoon white pepper
800g (1 lb 12oz) cold cooked sticky rice
4 tablespoons soy sauce
1 tablespoon toasted sesame oil
1 teaspoon salt, or to taste
Pinch of sugar

TO FINISH
Toasted sesame oil
Fresh coriander, finely chopped
Chilli oil
Lime juice
Peanuts (optional)

1 Heat the ghee or vegetable oil in a heavy-based frying pan and fry the garlic and ginger for 3–4 minutes. Add the peas and carrots and cook until tender, 4–5 minutes. Add the paneer and cook for 2–3 minutes, until lightly golden. Stir in the white pepper and spring onions and cook for 1 minute.

2 Add the rice, soy sauce, sesame oil, salt and sugar. Toss well until the rice is thoroughly heated through and fragrant.

3 Drizzle over some more sesame oil and sprinkle with the coriander, chilli oil, a squeeze of lime and peanuts, if using.

SERVES: 4 • PREP TIME: 10 MINUTES • COOK TIME: 40 MINUTES

Gochujang, Chickpea & Aubergine Traybake

You can't really beat a good traybake, and this one is brilliant – spicy, tangy and satisfying. If it's a little salty or dry, just add a splash of water to the tray and toss well. It'll bring everything back to life.

1 large aubergine, cut into cubes, lightly salted then left in a colander for 10–15 minutes to draw out its moisture
1 head of broccoli, cut into small florets
1 x 400-g (14-oz) can chickpeas, drained
4 shallots, halved
200g (7oz) paneer, cut into chunky 3-cm (1¼-inch) cubes
80g spinach (optional)

FOR THE SAUCE
1 tablespoon soy sauce
2 tablespoons gochujang (red chilli paste)
1½ tablespoons sesame oil
1 tablespoon olive oil
1 tablespoon honey
1 tablespoon rice wine vinegar
1 tablespoon lime juice
2 teaspoons garlic, crushed or finely chopped
2 teaspoons ginger, finely grated

TO FINISH
Fresh coriander, finely chopped
Spring onions, finely sliced
Peanut butter
Lime juice
Roasted peanuts, roughly chopped

1. Preheat the oven to 220°C (425°F), Gas Mark 7. Line a large baking tray with nonstick baking paper.
2. First make the sauce: in a bowl, whisk together all the ingredients for it. Add 1–2 tablespoons of water, if needed – the mixture should be spoonable, but not watery. Taste and adjust as necessary – it should be salty, sweet, tangy and punchy.
3. Rinse the aubergine, drain well, then place in a large bowl. Add the aubergine, broccoli, chickpeas and shallots and toss together. Add just over half the sauce and toss well to coat.
4. Spread the vegetables on the prepared tray in a single layer, as overcrowding will cause them to steam rather than roast. Place in the oven for 20 minutes, until the aubergine starts to soften.
5. Reserve 1 tablespoon of the sauce, then toss the paneer in the remainder. Remove the tray from the oven, nestle the paneer among the vegetables and return to the oven for a further 15 minutes, until the paneer has golden edges. The sauce should look sticky and caramelized, and the shallots soft and jammy.
6. Scatter the spinach, if using, over the hot vegetables in the tray. Return to the oven for 1–2 minutes, just until the spinach is lightly wilted.
7. To finish, sprinkle with the coriander, spring onions, peanuts and a generous squeeze of fresh lime juice.
8. To make a quick dressing, add the reserved tablespoon of sauce to the sticky residue in the bottom of the tray, then loosen it with a little water. Add peanut butter and lime juice.
9. Serve with rice, plenty of dressing and a sprinkle of roasted peanuts.

SERVES: 2 • PREP TIME: 10 MINUTES • COOK TIME: 10 MINUTES

Banh Mi

Everyone loves this Vietnamese classic, and here it is, reworked. Think punchy marinades, crunchy pickles and fresh herbs – all the good stuff. Paneer works perfectly here, soaking up flavour while holding its shape. This sandwich is a firm favourite in my lunch rotation.

200g (7oz) All the Aunties Cumin, Chilli & Turmeric Paneer, cut into 8 slices
1 large baguette, or 2 smaller bake-at-home baguettes
1 tablespoon Sriracha
1 tablespoon mayonnaise
Neutral oil, for frying

FOR THE MARINADE
1 teaspoon sesame oil
1 tablespoon hoisin sauce
1 teaspoon tomato ketchup
1 teaspoon garam masala or curry powder
1 teaspoon garlic-ginger paste

FOR THE SALAD
90g (3oz) red or white cabbage, grated
6 radishes, finely chopped
1 carrot, grated
Zest and juice of 1 lime
¼ teaspoon salt
½ teaspoon sugar
Handful of fresh coriander, roughly chopped
Handful of fresh mint, roughly chopped (optional)

1. Preheat the oven to 180°C (350°F), Gas Mark 4.
2. Combine the marinade ingredients in a bowl and mix well.
3. Score the paneer lightly and add to the marinade. Leave for 5–10 minutes.
4. Meanwhile, put the baguette in the oven for 5–7 minutes to warm through.
5. Combine the Sriracha and mayonnaise in a small bowl to make a spicy dressing, then set aside.
6. For the salad, combine the cabbage, radishes and carrot in a bowl, then add the lime juice and zest. Add the salt and sugar, then stir in the chopped coriander, reserving a little for the garnish.
7. Heat a little neutral oil in a frying pan, add the paneer and fry over a medium heat for 1–2 minutes on each side, until golden and charred.
8. Slice open the baguette and spread most of the dressing inside. Layer in the paneer and salad, then top with the remaining dressing, coriander and mint, if using, before serving.

SERVES: 2 • PREP TIME: 10 MINUTES • COOK TIME: 10 MINUTES

Paneer Bhurji

Also known as masala paneer scramble – finely crumbled paneer cooked with spices and aromatics – this dish is a staple of the paneer repertoire. Serve with rotli, pav or toast.

200g (7oz) All the Aunties Cumin, Chilli & Turmeric Paneer (brought up to room temperature before use)
1 tablespoon neutral oil
½ teaspoon cumin seeds
1 onion, finely chopped
1 teaspoon salt
1 tablespoon ginger-garlic paste
¼ teaspoon ground cumin
¼ teaspoon ground turmeric
¼ teaspoon chilli powder
¼ teaspoon ground coriander
¼ teaspoon amchur (mango powder), for a slight tang (optional)
1 tomato, finely diced (or 1 teaspoon tomato purée mixed with 2 tablespoons water)
Handful of frozen peas
1 teaspoon garam masala
Handful of spinach
Toasted bread, to serve

TO GARNISH
Lime juice
Fresh coriander, chopped
½ teaspoon kasoori methi (dried fenugreek leaves), crushed (optional)

1 Crumble the paneer and set aside. You should do this at room temperature.

2 Heat the oil in a heavy-based frying pan over a medium heat. Add the cumin seeds and let them sizzle for a few seconds. Add the onion and salt and cook until softened.

3 Add the ginger-garlic paste and cook for 1–2 mins until fragrant. Add the ground cumin, turmeric, chilli powder and ground coriander.

4 Add in your chopped tomatoes (or tomato purée and water if using), and cook for 2-3 minutes until broken down.

5 Stir in the peas and cook until tender.

6 Add in the crumbled paneer and garam masala. Toss everything together until heated through, then fold in the spinach and about 2 tablespoons of water, to soften the mix.

7 Finish with a generous squeeze of lime, chopped coriander and kasoori methi, if using.

8 Serve on hot toasted bread.

SERVES: 2 • PREP TIME: 10 MINUTES • COOK TIME: 25 MINUTES

Curry Leaf, Lemon & Cashew Scramble

My mum's South Indian rice dish with mustard seeds, curry leaves, cashews and lemon is fresh, moreish and regularly requested. I thought it could work with paneer and, lo and behold, it was indeed perfect. This is a treat with rice and noodles, or piled onto toast on a Saturday morning.

200g (7oz) paneer, at room temperature
1½ tablespoons neutral oil, or ghee for extra flavour
1 tablespoon raw cashews (or other nuts), halved
1 teaspoon mustard seeds
1 teaspoon urad dal (black lentils; optional but add a nice texture)
10–12 fresh curry leaves
1 onion, finely chopped
¼ teaspoon asafoetida
2½–3-cm (1–1¼-inch) piece of fresh root ginger, finely grated
1–2 green chillies, slit lengthways (deseed if you want less heat)
¼ teaspoon ground turmeric
Salt, to taste
2 tablespoons lemon juice
Finely chopped fresh coriander
Buttered toast, to serve

1. Crumble the paneer (best done at room temperature) and set aside.
2. Heat the oil or ghee in a wide frying pan over a medium heat. Add the cashews and fry until lightly golden, then remove and set aside.
3. In the same oil, add the mustard seeds and let them pop. Add the urad dal (if using) and toast until pale golden. Add the curry leaves (they should crackle). Now add the chopped onion and cook until softened.
4. Stir in the asafoetida, ginger and green chillies. Cook for 30–40 seconds, until fragrant but not browned. Asafoetida burns easily, so stir quickly.
5. Add the turmeric and salt, stirring quickly so the turmeric blooms but doesn't burn.
6. Add the crumbled paneer and gently fold through. Cook over a medium–low heat for 2–3 minutes, just until warmed through – the paneer should stay soft and fluffy.
7. Turn off the heat. Add the lemon juice and fried cashews. Taste and adjust the seasoning. Fold through the coriander.
8. Serve on top of generously buttered toast.

SERVES: 2 • PREP TIME: 15 MINUTES • COOK TIME: 5 MINUTES

Souvlaki

Halloumi works well in souvlaki (kebabs) as a meat substitute, but this version requires no skewers. It is also milder and less salty than the traditional version, so more family-friendly. The subtle taste of paneer also gives you a bit more room to play with when layering flavours on top. I personally love a dash of Tabasco, although it may be controversial here!

200g (7oz) All the Aunties Garlic & Herb Paneer (100g/3½ oz per wrap), cut into bite-sized cubes
2 flour wraps or large pittas

FOR THE MARINADE
1 tablespoon olive oil
3-4 garlic cloves, crushed or finely chopped
1 teaspoon oregano
½ teaspoon thyme
1 teaspoon honey
¾ teaspoon salt
½ teaspoon chilli flakes

FOR THE TZATZIKI
3 tablespoons Greek yogurt
1 garlic clove, crushed or finely chopped
¼ cucumber, seeds removed, coarsely grated
1–2 teaspoons lemon juice and zest of 1 lemon
¼ teaspoon salt
¼ tablespoon olive oil
Small handful of chopped dill

FOR THE SALAD
¼ cucumber, roughly chopped
1 tomato, roughly chopped
Handful of parsley, roughly chopped
¼ red onion, finely chopped
½ tablespoon olive oil
Pinch of salt

1. First make the marinade: in a medium bowl, whisk together the olive oil, garlic, oregano, thyme, honey, salt and chilli flakes for the marinade.
2. Add the paneer to the marinade. Toss well until evenly coated.
3. Heat a heavy-based frying pan over a medium heat. Add the marinated paneer and cook for 3–4 minutes, turning occasionally, until golden and lightly crisp on the outside.
4. Make the tzatziki by combining all the ingredients for it in a small bowl. Stir well and set aside.
5. In another bowl, toss the salad ingredients together.
6. Warm the wraps if you wish – either in a dry pan or an oven.
7. To assemble the souvlaki, spread some tzatziki over each wrap, add the warm paneer and a spoonful of salad, then fold or roll up to serve.

SERVES: 4 • PREP TIME: 40 MINUTES (INCLUDING 30 MINUTES MARINATING) • COOK TIME: 10 MINUTES

Spicy Miso Burgers

If you have vegetarian guests coming to your barbecue, fear not. Barbecued paneer is elite – on a par with any meat options, and never a compromise. It chars wonderfully, has a moist texture and absorbs flavours beautifully.

400g (14oz) paneer, cut into 8 squares (about 2cm/¾inch thick)
4 brioche burger buns
2 tablespoons Pickled Red Onion (see page 111), to serve (optional)
Fresh coriander, roughly chopped, to serve (optional)

FOR THE MARINADE
2 tablespoons white miso paste
1 tablespoon gochujang (red chilli paste)
2 tablespoons clear honey
2 teaspoons light soy sauce (reduced salt)
1 tablespoon neutral oil
1 teaspoon toasted sesame oil
1 tablespoon rice vinegar or lime juice
2 garlic cloves, crushed or finely grated
2-cm (¾-inch) piece of fresh root ginger, grated
½ teaspoon pepper

FOR THE KEWPIE-STYLE MAYO
4 tablespoons mayonnaise
1 teaspoon rice vinegar
½ teaspoon sugar
½ teaspoon Dijon mustard
Squeeze of lime juice (optional)

FOR THE SLAW
90g (3oz) white cabbage, finely shredded
2 spring onions, finely sliced
1 tablespoon rice vinegar
Pinch of salt

1. First make the marinade: in a bowl, whisk together all the ingredients for it until smooth and glossy. The marinade should be thick but brushable.

2. Lightly score the surface of each paneer square in a criss-cross pattern, then lay them on a tray. Reserve 1 tablespoon of the marinade, then brush the rest generously on both sides of the paneer. Leave to marinate for at least 30 minutes or up to 4 hours in the refrigerator.

3. To make the Kewpie-style mayo, mix the mayonnaise with rice vinegar, sugar, mustard and a squeeze of lime, if using. Whisk until smooth and slightly tangy. Chill until needed.

4. For the slaw, place the cabbage and spring onions in a separate bowl, then toss with the rice vinegar and salt. Set aside until needed. The slaw should remain crisp and lightly dressed.

5. Heat a griddle pan or barbecue until medium hot. The sugars in the marinade can burn, so avoid very high heat. Lightly oil the pan or barbecue rack, then add the paneer and cook for 3–4 minutes on each side, until it develops deep golden grill marks and the glaze becomes sticky and caramelized. In the final minute of cooking, brush the paneer with the reserved marinade for extra gloss. Remove from the heat and rest for 2 minutes.

6. Lightly toast the brioche buns, cut-side down, until golden. Set out the pickled red onion, if using.

7. To assemble, spread a generous layer of the Kewpie-style mayo over the base of each bun. Place two pieces of hot miso paneer on top. Add the pickled red onions, if using, followed by the cabbage and spring onion slaw. Finish with fresh coriander if you wish, then close with the top bun and press gently. Serve immediately while the paneer is hot and glossy and the slaw is crisp.

SERVES: 2 • PREP TIME: 10 MINUTES • COOK TIME: 8 MINUTES

Pizza Toast

This really does taste like pizza. Paneer is soft and milky, so it works perfectly in place of mozzarella while doubling up as protein. Pair it with a good marinara, some garlicky bread and a decent pesto, piled high on a good slice of toast. Simple, satisfying and impossible to get wrong.

Olive oil
2 slices sourdough bread
1 small garlic clove, halved
200g (7oz) paneer, cut into small cubes
350g (12½oz) marinara sauce, homemade (see below) or from a jar
Pesto, loosened with a little water if necessary (optional)
Sea salt flakes
Fresh basil (optional)

FOR THE HOMEMADE MARINARA
1 tablespoon olive oil
4 garlic cloves, finely sliced
1 x 400-g (14-oz) can good-quality chopped tomatoes
Pinch of sugar
Salt, to taste
Handful of fresh basil (optional)

1. If making your own marinara, heat the olive oil in a pan over a low heat and fry the garlic until just fragrant. Add the tomatoes, sugar and salt and simmer for 10–15 minutes until thickened. Stir through the basil, if using.
2. Heat a frying pan with a little olive oil and toast the sourdough on both sides until golden.
3. While the toast is still hot, rub the cut garlic clove over one side of it. Set aside.
4. Fry the paneer in the same pan for 1–2 minutes, until lightly golden. Add the marinara sauce and simmer until it thickens and clings to the paneer.
5. Spoon the paneer and sauce over the toast.
6. Add dabs of pesto, if using, a drizzle of olive oil, some flaky salt and fresh basil, if you like.

SERVES: 2 • PREP TIME: 15 MINUTES • COOK TIME: 5 MINUTES

The Ultimate Bombay Sandwich

You'll find a Bombay sandwich around every corner in India. Every version includes a generous amount of chutney, red onion and tomato. Double up on Cheddar if you want it extra gooey.

4 slices of soft white sandwich bread
Soft salted butter (optional)
2 tablespoons Coriander Chutney (see page 168)
2 tablespoons Garlic & Chilli Chutney (optional, see page 168), or ketchup mixed with chilli sauce for less heat

FOR THE VEGETABLE FILLING
½ cucumber, thinly sliced (optional)
1 firm tomato, thinly sliced
¼ red onion, very thinly sliced
1–2 teaspoons lemon juice
½ teaspoon ground cumin
Pinch of chaat masala (optional)
Salt, to taste

FOR THE PANEER MIX
200g (7oz) paneer or All the Aunties Cumin, Chilli & Turmeric Paneer, finely crumbled
50g (1¾oz) Cheddar cheese, grated
1 tablespoon soft butter or mayonnaise
1 green chilli, very finely chopped (deseed if you want less heat)
1 tablespoon chopped fresh coriander
Squeeze of lemon juice
Salt, to taste

ADDITIONAL FOLD-INS
(1–2 max; optional)
2 tablespoons finely grated carrot
2 tablespoons sweetcorn, well drained
2 tablespoons deseeded and finely diced red or green bell pepper

1 First make the filling: place the cucumber, tomato and red onion in a small bowl. Add the lemon juice, cumin, chaat masala if using, and salt to taste. Toss gently then leave to sit for 5 minutes so the onion softens slightly. When making the sandwich, pat the vegetables with kitchen paper to help prevent the bread from becoming soggy.

2 Place the crumbled paneer and grated Cheddar in a bowl. Add the butter, chilli, coriander, lemon juice and salt. Mix thoroughly until the mixture holds together when pressed with a spoon, but still feels fluffy. If using any optional fold-ins (carrot, sweetcorn or pepper), stir them through now. Keep the additions small and finely chopped so the mixture stays cohesive and easy to spread. Taste and adjust seasoning.

3 Lay out the bread slices on a board. Spread a thin, even layer of butter on one side of each slice (this step is optional but adds richness and helps the bread to toast evenly). Spread the coriander chutney generously over the buttered side of 1 slice.

4 Arrange the cucumber, if using, in a single layer on top of the chutney, slightly overlapping them. Follow with the tomato slices, then the onion. Keep the layers even so the sandwich presses together neatly.

5 Spoon the paneer mixture over the vegetables and spread it gently to the edges. Press lightly so it settles into the vegetables below. If using the garlic and chilli chutney, spread over the other slice of bread.

6 Place the remaining bread slices on top, chutney-side down. Press gently with your hands to help the sandwich hold together during toasting.

7 Heat a sandwich press or toastie maker, or a heavy-based frying pan over a medium heat. Toast the sandwich until the bread is golden and crisp on the outside and the filling is warmed through, about 3–5 minutes, depending on your method. If using a pan, press lightly with a spatula and flip once halfway through.

8 Remove from the heat and let the sandwich sit for about 30 seconds before cutting. Slice into halves and serve immediately while hot and crisp.

SERVES: 2 • PREP TIME: 25 MINUTES • COOK TIME: 10 MINUTES

Smoked Aubergine Raita & Paneer Pittas

If you make one thing from this dish, make the raita. It's a total game-changer, and my mum's famous recipe. Here the creamy, smoky tang couples perfectly with the paneer and crunchy slaw.

200g (7oz) paneer, cut into 1cm (½inch) thick sticks
1 tablespoon olive oil
1½ teaspoons za'atar or ground cumin
1–2 tablespoons lemon juice
Salt
Warm pittas, to serve

FOR THE RAITA
1 large aubergine
250g (9oz) thick Greek yogurt
1 teaspoon ground cumin
1 small garlic clove, crushed or finely grated
½ teaspoon sumac
1 teaspoon pomegranate molasses or clear honey, to taste
1–2 tablespoons lemon juice (to taste)
2 spring onions, finely sliced
Small handful of fresh coriander or mint, chopped

FOR THE SLAW
70g (2½ oz) red cabbage, finely shredded
1 small carrot, grated or julienned
½ red onion, very finely sliced
Small handful of fresh mint, finely sliced
Small handful of fresh coriander, finely sliced
1 tablespoon lemon juice
1 teaspoon olive oil
Pinch of salt

FOR THE TAHINI DRESSING
2 tablespoons tahini
1 tablespoon lemon juice
1 small garlic clove, crushed
1 teaspoon honey

1. Toss the paneer in a bowl with the olive oil, za'atar or cumin, salt and lemon juice. Turn gently so the pieces are evenly coated. Set aside.
2. Char the aubergine directly over a flame or under a hot grill until blackened and soft. Transfer to a bowl and cover and leave to steam for about 10 minutes.
3. Once cool enough to handle, peel off and discard the charred skin. Roughly chop or mash the flesh.
4. In a bowl mix the warm aubergine with the yogurt, cumin, garlic, sumac, pomegranate molasses, salt and lemon juice. Fold in the spring onions and coriander. Taste and adjust the seasoning. Set aside.
5. To make the slaw, combine all the ingredients in a bowl, add a pinch of salt and toss together. Set aside.
6. Whisk together the dressing ingredients with a pinch of salt. Gradually whisk in 1–2 tablespoons of cold water, a little at a time, until the dressing becomes smooth, creamy and spoonable.
7. Heat a frying pan over a medium–high heat. Add the paneer and cook for 2–3 minutes per side, until golden and lightly crisp.
8. To assemble the wraps, spread a spoonful of tahini dressing inside each pitta. Add a generous spoonful of the aubergine raita and tuck in the warm paneer sticks. Finish with a handful of slaw and serve immediately.

SERVES: 2 • PREP TIME: 10 MINUTES • COOK TIME: 5–7 MINUTES

Edamame, Tahini & Chilli Oil Toast

Do you ever feel like just eating chilli crisp straight from the jar? Spicy, salty and aromatic, it's completely addictive. This recipe has the same effect. Crispy paneer and loads of chilli oil, piled onto toast, while the edamame spread cools things down just enough.

1 tablespoon neutral oil
200g (7oz) paneer, crumbled
Masala chilli crisp (see page 171) or chilli oil, to taste
150g (5½oz) frozen edamame beans, defrosted
1 tablespoon tahini
1 teaspoon white miso
½ teaspoon honey
1 tablespoon olive oil
2 slices of bread, toasted
1 small garlic clove, halved
Fresh coriander, roughly chopped
Pickled Red Onion (see page 111)
Crushed roasted peanuts
Salt

1. Heat the oil in a heavy-based frying pan over a medium heat. Fry the paneer until golden and crisp. Toss in the chilli crisp while hot. Set aside.
2. Using a blender or food processor, blitz the edamame, tahini, miso, honey, olive oil and a pinch of salt until smooth and thick, like hummus. Add a splash of water if needed to loosen.
3. Toast the bread until golden, then rub each slice lightly with the cut side of the garlic.
4. Spread a generous layer of the edamame mixture over the toast.
5. Top with the chilli crisp paneer.
6. Sprinkle with some coriander, pickled red onions and crushed peanuts, then drizzle with extra chilli oil or chilli crisp.

SERVES: 4 • PREP TIME: 20 MINUTES, PLUS MARINATION • COOK TIME: 12 MINUTES

Katti Roll

Picnic food doesn't get much better than this: a paratha wrap loaded with paneer, vegetables and smothered in egg. Need I say more?

2 tablespoons thick yogurt
1 tablespoon ginger-garlic paste
1 teaspoon Kashmiri (mild) chilli powder
½ teaspoon ground turmeric
1 teaspoon ground cumin
1 teaspoon ground coriander
½ teaspoon garam masala
1 teaspoon chaat masala
1 tablespoon lemon juice
2 tablespoons neutral oil plus extra for frying
400g (14oz) paneer, cut into 2-cm (¾-inch) strips
1 large onion, sliced
1 green bell pepper, deseeded and thinly sliced
Squeeze of lemon juice
Salt

TO SERVE
4 parathas
4 eggs
Coriander Chutney and Madhu's Garlic & Chilli Chutney (see page 168)
1 red onion, very thinly sliced or pickled (see page 111)
1 teaspoon chaat masala
Roughly chopped coriander
Squeeze of lemon juice

1. Combine the yogurt, ginger-garlic paste, spices, lemon juice, oil and salt, to taste, in a bowl. Add the paneer strips and gently coat. Cover and leave to marinate for up to 30 minutes.

2. Heat 1 tablespoon neutral oil in a heavy-based frying pan over a medium–high heat. Arrange the paneer in a single layer and cook undisturbed for 2–3 minutes until lightly charred. Turn and cook the other side, then add the onion and green pepper. Cook for a further 2–3 minutes until the vegetables soften slightly but still have some bite, and the paneer is coated in the thick masala. Finish with a squeeze of lemon. Remove from the heat.

3. Heat a pan over a medium heat. Cook each paratha in a dry pan until golden on both sides.

4. For authentic Kolkata style, lightly beat one of the eggs and pour it into the hot pan, spreading it into a thin layer. Immediately place a cooked paratha on top so it sticks to the egg. Cook until set, then flip briefly to warm through. Repeat with an egg for each paratha, if desired.

5. Spread the coriander chutney across the egg side of the paratha and drizzle with garlic and chilli chutney. Pile the hot paneer mixture down the centre. Top with some red onion, a sprinkle of chaat masala and coriander and a squeeze of lemon.

6. Roll the paratha tightly from the bottom, wrapping the lower half in parchment or foil to hold the filling. Serve immediately while the paneer is hot and the paratha is crisp.

SERVES: 4 AS A SIDE • PREP TIME: 20 MINUTES • COOK TIME: 20 MINUTES

Paneer Paratha

Stuffed breads are one of life's great joys – I grew up watching my grandma make them for breakfast each weekend. To me they are the greatest snack in existence. Paneer works brilliantly in paratha as it doesn't melt, so holds up really well. In India it's very common to take in paratha and pickle for a work lunch – see you later meal deal sandwiches!

These freeze really well, so make a batch and keep it in the freezer to reheat when needed.

1 teaspoon neutral oil, for tempering and frying
1 teaspoon black mustard seeds
¼ teaspoon asafoetida
400g (14oz) paneer, grated or crumbled
2 green chillies, finely chopped (deseed if you want less heat)
Handful of fresh coriander, finely chopped
¾ teaspoon fresh root ginger, grated
½ teaspoon red chilli powder
½ teaspoon ground coriander
½ teaspoon garam masala
1 tablespoon lime juice
1 teaspoon salt (or to taste)
½–1 small boiled potato, mashed (optional, for binding)
1 tablespoon of breadcrumbs, if needed (optional, for binding)
Yogurt and chutney, to serve

FOR THE TRADITIONAL DOUGH
125g (4½oz) wholemeal flour
Pinch of salt
1 tablespoon neutral oil
125ml (4fl oz) warm water

FOR A QUICK DOUGH ALTERNATIVE
125g (4½oz) self-raising flour
175g (6oz) thick Greek yogurt
Pinch of salt

1. To temper the spices (optional but recommended), heat a small splash of oil in a pan. Add the mustard seeds and allow them to pop, then stir in the asafoetida and grated ginger. Remove from the heat and let cool slightly.
2. Prepare the filling by combining the paneer, chillies and fresh coriander in a bowl. Add the ground coriander, chilli powder, garam masala, lime juice and salt. Stir in the tempered spices and mashed potato, if using. The mixture should be moist but not wet. If it feels loose, add a little more mashed potato or a spoonful of breadcrumbs.
3. To make the traditional dough, mix the flour, salt and oil in a bowl. Gradually add the measured warm water and knead into a soft, pliable dough. Cover and rest for 20–30 minutes.
4. If making the quick dough alternative, mix the flour, yogurt and salt until a soft dough forms (add a little more flour if sticky). Rest for 5–10 minutes. The result will be slightly softer and fluffier than a traditional paratha, but just as delicious.
5. Divide the dough into golf ball-sized portions. Gently flatten the ball, dust lightly with flour and roll each into a small circle, about 10–12cm (4–4½in) wide. Place 2 tablespoons of filling in the centre. Bring the edges together over the filling and pinch to seal. Gently flatten again and roll into a paratha, taking care not to integrate the paneer filling into the dough; you need enough filling in the centre to ensure it is properly stuffed.
6. Heat a little oil in a heavy-based frying pan over a medium heat. Cook each paratha for 2–3 minutes per side, until golden and lightly puffed. Add a little extra oil for each paratha.
7. Serve hot with yogurt and chutney.

SERVES: 4 • PREP TIME: 20 MINUTES • COOK TIME: 12 MINUTES

Paneer Shawarma

We love a build-your-own meal in our house, and this is perfect for it. Warm spices, lots of sauces and paneer that soaks it all up. Great for feeding a crowd.

2 tablespoons thick Greek yogurt
1 tablespoon olive oil
1 tablespoon lemon juice
3 garlic cloves, grated
1 teaspoon ground cumin
1 teaspoon ground coriander
1 teaspoon smoked paprika
1 teaspoon dried oregano
½ teaspoon ground turmeric
½ teaspoon ground cinnamon
½ teaspoon ground allspice or mixed spice (optional)
½ teaspoon pepper
¾–1 teaspoon salt
400g (14oz) paneer, cut into thin strips

FOR THE QUICK PICKLED RED ONION

1 red onion, thinly sliced
2 tablespoons lemon juice
Pinch of salt
Pinch of sugar

FOR THE DRESSING

200g (7oz) Greek yogurt
1 small garlic clove, crushed or finely grated
1 tablespoon tahini (optional but excellent)
1 tablespoon lemon juice
1 tablespoon olive oil
Salt, to taste

TO SERVE

4 large flatbreads or wraps
Shredded lettuce
Sliced tomato
Sliced cucumber
Fresh parsley
Chilli sauce (optional)

1. Make the marinade by combining the yogurt, olive oil and lemon juice in a bowl, then add the garlic, cumin, coriander, smoked paprika, oregano, turmeric, cinnamon, all-spice, if using, pepper and salt. Add the paneer and coat gently but thoroughly. Leave to marinate for at least 10–15 minutes while you prepare the rest of the ingredients.
2. To make the pickle, toss the onion with the lemon juice, salt and sugar. Set aside – it will soften and turn bright pink.
3. To make the dressing, whisk the yogurt, garlic, tahini, if using, lemon juice and olive oil in a bowl. Season with salt to taste. The sauce should be creamy but pourable.
4. Heat a heavy-based frying pan or griddle pan over a medium–high heat. Arrange the paneer in a single layer and cook for 3–4 minutes, or until golden with lightly charred edges. Turn and cook the other side. Don't move it too early – you want a good colour.
5. Warm the flatbreads in a dry pan or directly over a flame for softness.
6. Spread some dressing over each flatbread. Add some lettuce, tomato and cucumber. Top with the hot shawarma paneer, followed by pickled red onions and parsley. Drizzle with any remaining dressing and chilli sauce, if using.
7. Roll up tightly and serve immediately.

SERVES: 4 • PREP TIME: 20 MINUTES • COOK TIME: 45 MINUTES

Roasted Aubergine, Cauliflower & Paneer Tart with Muhammara

I'm a sucker for anything spicy and nutty, and the muhammara in this recipe ticks both boxes. This began as me dipping paneer into whatever was in the fridge – and this particular choice was love at first bite. The combination has stuck and it's now a go-to crowd-pleaser.

1 small aubergine, cut into 2.5-cm (1-inch) cubes
½ small cauliflower, cut into florets
1 red onion, thickly sliced
3 tablespoons olive oil
1 teaspoon ground cumin
½ teaspoon chilli flakes
200g (7oz) paneer, sliced or torn into chunky pieces
1 sheet ready rolled all-butter puff pastry
Salt

FOR THE MUHAMMARA
1 large roasted red pepper, drained
40g (1½oz) walnuts
1 tablespoon pomegranate molasses
1 tablespoon olive oil
½ teaspoon ground cumin
Squeeze of lemon juice
Salt

FOR THE FRESH HERB TOPPING
Large handful of parsley, finely chopped
Small handful of mint, finely chopped
Large handful of rocket
¼ cucumber, finely chopped (optional)
1 tablespoon lemon juice
1 teaspoon lemon zest
1 tablespoon olive oil
Salt, to taste

TO SERVE
Pomegranate seeds
Extra drizzle of olive oil

1. Preheat the oven to 220°C (425°F), Gas Mark 7. In a large bowl, toss the aubergine, cauliflower and red onion with the olive oil, cumin, chilli flakes and ½ – 1 teaspoon salt. Spread onto a large baking tray in a single layer and set aside.

2. Line a second tray with baking paper and lay the puff pastry on it. Score a 2-cm (¾-inch) border around the edges, being careful not to cut all the way through. Lightly prick the central area with a fork.

3. Place both trays in the oven. Roast the vegetables for 20 minutes, until the aubergine is soft and starting to caramelize and the cauliflower is golden at the edges. Bake the pastry for 10 minutes, until it is starting to puff, then gently press down the centre and set aside.

4. After the vegetables have had 20 minutes, add the paneer pieces to the same tray and gently turn them in the residual oil and spices. Return to the oven for a further 8–10 minutes, until the paneer is lightly golden at the edges.

5. While everything is cooking, put the muhammara ingredients in a blender or food processor and blitz until thick, slightly textured and spreadable. It should feel like a loose pesto, not a sauce. If it is too wet, add a few more walnuts and blend again.

6. Once the vegetables are ready, spread the muhammara evenly over the pastry, leaving the border clear. Spoon the roasted vegetables and paneer over the pastry, distributing everything evenly without piling it too high. Return to the oven for 10–15 minutes, until the pastry is golden and crisp.

7. Meanwhile, combine the topping ingredients in a small bowl. Toss lightly.

8. Once the tart is out of the oven, let it sit for 5 minutes. Scatter over the herb topping, followed by pomegranate seeds and a light drizzle of olive oil. Slice and serve warm.

One-Pot Wonders

The power of a one-pot dish is something to behold. Maximum flavour, minimal washing up. Sometimes that is exactly what you need.

I grew up cooking with my mother, and still somehow managed to use every single pan in the kitchen for things that absolutely did not require it. She'd just watch as I pulled out another one, before eventually stepping in to teach me how to actually cook, properly, in one pot, so I got the flavour and texture without compromise. These are those recipes. Big flavours, much less chaos and far fewer pans.

SERVES: 2 • PREP TIME: 10 MINUTES • COOK TIME: 15 MINUTES

Vagharelo Rice

My Madhu Baa (grandma) doesn't really entertain food that isn't Indian. So when she comes to stay, I usually cook something simple and familiar for her – always under her supervision. Vagharelo rice is one of those dishes every Indian household claims as their own, and this is hers. I've added pine nuts – untraditional, and she'd probably have something to say about it – but I love the extra nuttiness they bring.

1½ tablespoons neutral oil
½ onion, finely chopped
3 garlic cloves, crushed or finely chopped
1 green chilli, finely chopped (deseed if you want less heat)
1 teaspoon cumin seeds
1 teaspoon black mustard seeds
5 curry leaves
¼ teaspoon asafoetida
200g (7oz) plain paneer or All the Aunties Cumin, Chilli & Turmeric Paneer
½ teaspoon turmeric (if using plain paneer)
300g (10½oz) cooked basmati rice (leftovers are fine)
2 teaspoons lightly ground pine nuts (optional)
Squeeze of lemon juice
Handful of fresh coriander, chopped, to finish
Pinch of sugar

1. In a medium–hot heavy-based frying pan, heat the oil and fry the onion, garlic and green chilli until soft.
2. Add the cumin and mustard seeds, the curry leaves and asafoetida, and cook until fragrant.
3. Crumble in the paneer, and fry for 2–3 minutes, until golden and slightly crisp. Sprinkle in the turmeric (if using plain paneer) and stir to combine.
4. Add the cooked rice and stir-fry until heated through.
5. Sprinkle with the pine nuts, lemon juice and coriander. Finally, add a pinch of sugar to taste – it's a very Gujarati touch.

SERVES: 4 • PREP TIME: 20 MINUTES • COOK TIME: 40 MINUTES

Peri-peri Traybake with Roasted Potatoes, Broccoli & Minty Peas

Homemade peri-peri sauce really isn't that hard to make, and it's unbelievably good. Plus, this is a one-tray wonder – perfect.

400g (14oz) paneer, torn into large chunks
500g (1lb 2oz) new potatoes, halved
3 tablespoons olive oil
1 large head of broccoli, or 250g Tenderstem broccoli, cut into florets
Salt and pepper
Squeeze of lemon juice
Garlic mayonnaise, to serve (optional)

FOR THE PERI-PERI SAUCE
2–4 red chillies, roughly chopped (deseed if you want less heat, and use 2 rather than 4)
4 garlic cloves
¼ red onion, roughly chopped
1 tablespoon lemon juice
1 tablespoon vinegar
2 tablespoons olive oil
1 teaspoon smoked paprika
½ teaspoon sweet paprika (optional)
½ teaspoon dried oregano
½ teaspoon sugar (optional)
1 teaspoon salt
½ teaspoon pepper

FOR THE MINTY PEAS
200–250g (7–9oz) frozen peas
Small handful of parsley, finely chopped
Small handful of mint, finely chopped
1 tablespoon lemon juice
Pinch of chilli flakes
Salt

1. Preheat the oven to 200°C (400°F), Gas Mark 6.
2. First make the peri-peri sauce: place all the ingredients for it in a blender or food processor and blitz until smooth. Set aside.
3. On a large baking tray, toss the potatoes with 2 tablespoons of the olive oil plus salt and pepper. Spread the potatoes on the tray, cut-side down and roast for 20 minutes.
4. Remove the tray and push the potatoes to one side. Add the broccoli and toss with a little oil and salt, then add paneer pieces. Brush or spoon half of the peri-peri sauce over the paneer. Return to the oven for 15–20 minutes. The paneer should be golden at the edges and slightly caramelized. If you want extra char, place under a hot grill for the last 3–4 minutes.
5. Add the frozen peas to the hot tray for the last 5 minutes of cooking. They will defrost and warm through in the oven.
6. Once out of the oven, sprinkle over the parsley, mint, lemon juice, chilli flakes and a pinch of salt. Give the peas a gentle toss on the tray, slightly smashing some for texture.
7. Cook down the remaining peri-peri sauce with some water to loosen, simmering for 5–10 minutes – you're working with raw garlic and chilli here. Drizzle the sauce over the tray then add a final squeeze of fresh lemon juice and a dollop of garlic mayonnaise, if you like, before serving straight from the tray.

SERVES: 4 • PREP TIME: 15 MINUTES • COOK TIME: 25 MINUTES

Fajita Traybake

An easy fajita recipe is a must-have. Paneer is wonderfully meaty, so it works perfectly in a fajita. The salsa and guac recipes aren't especially traditional, but are courtesy of Sima Aunty and well worth a try – we have a 100 percent conversion rate from sceptic to lover.

400g (14oz) paneer, cut into 2-cm (¾-in) strips
2 red onions, cut into thin wedges
3 bell peppers in mixed colours, deseeded and sliced
2 tablespoons neutral oil
Salt and pepper

FOR THE FAJITA SPICE MIX
2 teaspoons ground cumin
2 teaspoons smoked paprika
½–1 teaspoon cayenne pepper
2 teaspoons garlic granules
1 teaspoon dried oregano
1 teaspoon all-purpose seasoning, such as Aromat (optional)

FOR THE GUACAMOLE
2 ripe avocados
1 tablespoon lime juice, plus 1 lime cut into wedges
2 tablespoons finely chopped coriander
1 teaspoon juice from pickled jalapeños
1 garlic clove, crushed or finely chopped

FOR THE SALSA
2 tomatoes, finely chopped
1 tablespoon lime juice
1 tablespoon finely chopped coriander
½ teaspoon ground cumin
½ white onion, finely chopped
1 tablespoon pickled jalapeños, finely chopped

TO SERVE
8–12 tortillas
Soured cream
Grated Cheddar cheese

1 Preheat the oven to 220°C (425°F), Gas Mark 7.

2 Mix the fajita spice ingredients together in a small bowl.

3 Place the onion wedges and peppers on 1-2 trays, taking care not to overcrowd the trays and leaving room to add the paneer. Drizzle with the oil, sprinkle over the spice mix, and season with salt and pepper. Toss well to coat.

4 Roast on the top shelf of the oven for 10 minutes. Remove from the oven and add the paneer to the tray, then return to the oven to bake until the paneer is slightly golden and the peppers and onions are soft.

5 Meanwhile, make the guacamole. Mash the avocado flesh in a bowl with a fork and then add the lime juice, 1 tablespoon chopped coriander, the pickled jalapeño juice, garlic, salt and pepper. Mash again until combined.

6 For the salsa, combine the tomatoes in a another bowl with the lime juice, coriander, cumin, onion and jalapeños. Season to taste.

7 Wrap the tortillas in foil and place in the oven on a low shelf for the last 5 minutes of the vegetable roasting time to warm through. Alternatively, if you have a gas hob, lightly toast each tortilla directly over the flame, turning with metal tongs until lightly charred. Keep warm.

8 Scatter the remaining coriander over the traybake. Serve with the soured cream, guacamole and salsa, along with the warm tortillas.

SERVES: 4 • PREP TIME: 15 MINUTES • COOK TIME: 40 MINUTES

One-Pot Cauliflower, Pea & Paneer Biryani

I love a traditional biryani, but it's certainly a project. Here is the shortcut version – with all the flavour and far less effort. Packed with vegetables, protein and spice, this is comfort food that doesn't require a full day in the kitchen.

2 tablespoons neutral oil or ghee
1 small cauliflower, cut into small florets
1 bay leaf
3 green cardamom pods
1 black cardamom pod (or replace with another green cardamom pod)
4 cloves
1 cinnamon stick
2 teaspoons cumin seeds
1 large onion, finely chopped
3 tablespoons ginger-garlic paste
3 green chillies, slit lengthways (deseed if you want less heat)
2 tomatoes, finely chopped
1½ teaspoons turmeric
2 teaspoons biryani masala or garam masala
1 teaspoon ground coriander
1½ teaspoons fine salt (to taste)
300g (10½oz) paneer, cut into 2.5-cm (1-inch) cubes
140g (5oz) frozen peas
2 large handfuls of spinach
200g (7oz) basmati rice, rinsed and soaked for 20 minutes
500ml (18fl oz) hot water
Salt

TO SERVE
Small handful of finely chopped coriander
Small handful of fresh mint
1 tablespoon lemon juice
2 tablespoons yogurt (optional)

1. Heat 1 tablespoon of the oil in a heavy-based pan over a medium–high heat. Add the cauliflower florets with a pinch of salt and sauté for 4–5 minutes, until lightly golden at the edges but still firm. Remove and set aside.

2. In the same pan, heat the remaining oil or ghee then add the bay leaf, cardamom pods, cloves, cinnamon stick and cumin seeds and cook for 2 minutes, until fragrant. Add the onion and cook for around 5 minutes until soft and lightly golden. Stir in the ginger-garlic paste and green chillies. Cook for 1 minute.

3. Add the tomatoes and cook for 4–5 minutes until softened and the mixture thickens slightly.

4. Stir in turmeric, biryani masala, ground coriander and salt.

5. Add the paneer cubes and sauté gently for 2–3 minutes so they are coated in the masala. Return the sautéed cauliflower to the pan and add the peas. Stir gently to combine.

6. Drain the soaked rice well and add it to the pan. Mix carefully so the grains remain intact but are evenly coated.

7. Pour in the hot water and bring to a gentle boil. Taste the liquid – it should be slightly saltier than you expect, as the rice will absorb it. Cover tightly, reduce the heat to low and cook for 15 minutes, without stirring.

8. Turn off the heat, scatter spinach over the rice, cover again and rest for 10 minutes. The residual heat will wilt the spinach and finish cooking the rice.

9. Uncover and gently fluff the rice with a fork. Finish with the chopped coriander, mint, lemon juice and a spoonful of yogurt, if using.

SERVES: 4 • PREP TIME: 15 MINUTES • COOK TIME: 35 MINUTES

Butter Bean, Salsa Verde & Cherry Tomato Traybake

Beans are having a moment – and quite rightly. I grew up on them, and now they form a key part of a balanced diet. This dish has it all – carbohydrates, protein, fibre and good fats. It's firmly in my rotation. The punchy salsa verde lifts the dish into something really special, so don't skip it.

400g (14oz) All the Aunties Garlic & Herb Paneer, cut into large cubes
1 large red onion, cut into wedges
400-g (14-oz) can chickpeas, drained
200g (7oz) Tenderstem broccoli or green beans (cut in half, if thick)
3 tablespoons olive oil
1 teaspoon dried oregano
1 teaspoon chilli flakes (optional)
400g (14oz) can cherry or plum tomatoes (plus a few fresh cherry tomatoes, if you like)
400-g (14-oz) can butter beans (or cannellini), plus their liquid
4–6 garlic cloves, crushed or finely sliced
Zest of 1 lemon
Salt and pepper

FOR THE SALSA VERDE
Large handful of fresh parsley, finely chopped
Small handful of basil, finely chopped (or parsley, coriander or dill)
1 small garlic clove, crushed or very finely chopped
1 tablespoon finely chopped capers
1 tablespoon finely chopped gherkins or jalapeños from a jar (optional)
1–2 anchovy fillets, finely chopped (optional)
1 tablespoon red wine vinegar or lemon juice
4–5 tablespoons extra-virgin olive oil
Salt and pepper

1 Preheat the oven to 220°C (425°F), Gas Mark 7. Add the paneer, red onion wedges, chickpeas and tenderstem broccoli to a large, high-sided roasting tray. Drizzle with about 2½ tablespoons of the olive oil and scatter over the oregano, chilli flakes, salt and pepper. Toss everything gently but thoroughly, so it is evenly coated, then spread into a single layer.

2 Roast for 15 minutes, until the paneer is lightly golden at the edges, the chickpeas start to crisp and the broccoli is lightly charred at the tips. This stage builds flavour and ensures proper roasting rather than steaming.

3 Remove the tray from the oven and add the tomatoes plus the butter beans with their liquid. Scatter over the garlic and toss gently to combine, being careful not to break up the paneer too much.

4 Return the tray to the oven for a further 15–20 minutes, until the tomatoes have burst and collapsed, the butter bean liquid has reduced slightly and turned glossy, and everything looks saucy but not watery. You should see bubbling juices around the edges. If it looks too dry, add 1–2 tablespoons of hot water; if it looks too wet, give it another 5 minutes uncovered. Finish with the lemon zest and toss to distribute.

5 While the traybake cooks, make the salsa verde. Combine the parsley and basil in a bowl and mix in the garlic, capers, gherkins and anchovies, if using. Stir in the vinegar or lemon juice and the extra-virgin olive oil and season to taste. The salsa should be loose, glossy and sharp – bright enough to cut through the richness of the beans and paneer. Taste and adjust the seasoning.

6 Let the tray sit for 5 minutes once out of the oven. Spoon the traybake into bowls and drizzle the salsa verde generously over the top, or serve it separately for people to add themselves. Serve warm with crusty bread, rice or crispy potatoes to mop up the juices.

FIRE & SMOKE

SERVES: 3–4 • PREP TIME: 5 MINUTES • COOK TIME: 10 MINUTES

Hariyali Paneer Kebabs

This marinade is bright and herby, and I could happily eat it by the spoon. It works with anything, but is especially good with paneer. Leave it overnight if you can.

400g (14oz) paneer, cut into 8 chunky cubes (All the Aunties Cumin, Chilli & Turmeric Paneer works well)

FOR THE MARINADE

100g (3½oz) fresh coriander, stalks included
30g (1oz) fresh mint leaves
1–2 green chillies, to taste (deseed if you want less heat)
2 garlic cloves
2.5-cm (1-inch) piece of fresh root ginger, roughly chopped
1 teaspoon ground cumin
2 teaspoons lemon juice (or 1 teaspoon amchur)
1 teaspoon jaggery (Indian sweetener), clear honey or sugar
1 tablespoon thick Greek yogurt
1 tablespoon olive oil or ghee
½ teaspoon salt
1 tablespoon roasted peanuts

TO SERVE

Pickled Red Onions (see page 111)
Naans
Yogurt
Lime juice
Lettuce and cucumber

1. Make the marinade using a blender or food processor: blitz the coriander, mint, chillies, garlic, ginger, cumin, lemon juice (or amchur), jaggery or sugar, greek yogurt, oil, salt and roasted peanuts in a blender or food processor until smooth but still slightly textured. Transfer to a bowl.
2. Lightly score the paneer cubes then stir into the marinade. Cover and leave in the refrigerator for at least 1 hour, or overnight.
3. Preheat a grill or barbecue until very hot, or prepare your air fryer.
4. Thread the paneer onto skewers, leaving a little space between each piece.
5. Grill for 6–8 minutes, turning once or twice, until charred and fragrant, or barbecue until lightly blistered, about 2 minutes per side. Alternatively, air-fry at 180°C (350°F) for 8–10 minutes.
6. Serve with pickled red onion, naans, yogurt, a squeeze of lime and some lettuce and cucumber.

If using wooden skewers for your kebabs, soak them in water for 30 minutes before use to prevent burning.

SERVES: 4 • PREP TIME: 25 MINUTES • COOK TIME: 20 MINUTES

Kandhari Paneer Tikka

These are gorgeous – vibrant, pink and charred – with a tangy, mouthwatering marinade, all tied up with a sticky, fruity stuffing. The stuffing follows the same method as the Paneer Pasanda (see page 155), and it definitely requires the char to offset some of the tang from the pomegranate. It's brilliant on its own as a starter, but also goes well with rice as a main.

400–500g paneer, cut into large cubes or blocks
1 teaspoon oil or melted butter

FOR THE STUFFING
6–8 prunes, finely chopped
2 tablespoons cashews, finely chopped
Salt

FOR THE MARINADE
4 tablespoons thick Greek yogurt
2 teaspoons chickpea flour
1 tablespoon cashew paste (optional, but recommended for creaminess)
1 tablespoon finely grated beetroot
1–1½ tablespoons pomegranate molasses
1 tablespoon ginger-garlic paste
1 teaspoon Kashmiri (mild) chilli powder
½ teaspoon ground turmeric
1 teaspoon ground coriander
½ teaspoon ground cumin
½ teaspoon garam masala
Pinch of black pepper
1 teaspoon salt

FOR THE SALSA
1 tablespoon oil
1 teaspoon mustard seeds (or ½ teaspoon wholegrain mustard)
2 garlic cloves, finely grated or chopped
2 tomatoes, finely chopped
Pinch of chilli powder

TO SERVE
Steamed basmati rice
Lemon juice
Coriander, roughly chopped

1. Cut a horizontal slit into each piece of paneer, leaving a hinge still intact. Mix the prunes and cashews with a pinch of salt, then gently stuff inside the paneer.

2. In a bowl, combine all the marinade ingredients to form a thick, smooth, pink mixture. Coat the paneer evenly, taking care not to break it, and leave to marinate for at least 30 minutes, or ideally overnight in the fridge.

3. Preheat the oven to 200°C (400°F), Gas Mark 6, or heat a griddle or heavy-based frying pan. Cook the paneer for 8-10 minutes, until lightly charred on the edges and warmed through, turning once and brushing with a little oil or butter for a glossy finish.

4. To make the salsa, heat the oil in a pan and add the mustard seeds. Once they begin to pop, add the garlic and cook briefly until fragrant. Pour the hot oil over the tomatoes. Add the salt and chilli powder to taste and give it a good stir.

5. Serve the paneer tikka hot on a bed of rice, spooning over the tomato, garlic and mustard salsa. Finish with a squeeze of lemon juice and some chopped coriander.

SERVES: 4 • PREP TIME: 15 MINUTES (PLUS OPTIONAL CHILLING) • COOK TIME: 6–8 MINUTES

Garlic & Chilli Paneer Skewers

Aglio e Olio is my favourite pasta dish, and the first thing I ever learnt to cook. It's built on simple, punchy flavours: garlic gently fried in olive oil, chilli for heat and parsley for freshness. These skewers are inspired by those simple and delicious flavours. We all know that smell when garlic and chilli are frying, and this is that in a dish. There's plenty of both, with parsley and lemon to lift it, and breadcrumbs for a bit of texture.

400g (14oz) paneer, cut into large cubes and lightly scored
1 courgette, thickly sliced
1 red onion, cut into wedges and layers separated (optional)

TO FINISH
Flat-leaf parsley, finely chopped
Squeeze of lemon juice (optional)
Panko breadcrumbs, toasted (optional)

FOR THE GARLIC & CHILLI PASTE
5–6 garlic cloves
2–3 red chillies, roughly chopped (deseed if you want less heat)
2 tablespoons extra-virgin olive oil
½ teaspoon red wine vinegar or apple cider vinegar
Salt and black pepper
1 tablespoon butter, for basting

1. To make the paste, crush the garlic and chillies with salt into a coarse paste using a mortar and pestle or small blender. Slowly drizzle in olive oil to form a thick, clingy paste. Stir in the vinegar and season with black pepper. The paste should stick to the paneer without dripping.
2. If barbecuing, mix 1 tablespoon of the paste with the butter and set aside for basting.
3. Toss the paneer gently in the remaining paste until evenly coated, then cover and chill for 1–12 hours. Remove 20–30 minutes before cooking.
4. Lightly season the courgette and onion, if using, with salt and a tiny drizzle of oil. Thread the paneer onto skewers, alternating with vegetables, if using.
5. Barbecue over a medium-high heat, turning every 2 minutes, for 6–8 minutes, and basting now and then with the reserved paste. Alternatively, cook undisturbed in a hot griddle pan or heavy-based frying pan for 2–3 minutes per side. Or air-fry at 190°C (370°F) for 7–8 minutes. When done, the paneer should be lightly charred and the vegetables al dente.
6. Finish with a squeeze of lemon juice, the parsley and toasted breadcrumbs, if using.
7. Serve hot with salad or fresh bread.

If using panko breadcrumbs, add 1 teaspoon of the reserved marinade before toasting to turn them into a deliciously spicy and garlicky topping.

MAKES: 4 KEBABS • PREP TIME: 40 MINUTES (INCLUDING MARINATION) • COOK TIME: 15 MINUTES

Soy & Honey Paneer with Spring Onion & Shiitake

This dish looks pretty, is very easy to prep and is guaranteed to be the belle of the ball at your barbecue. I recommend prepping a batch in advance and then laying them out for grilling. Serve hot on top of Sticky Paneer Fried Rice (see page 84) or with a salad.

300g Tenderstem or purple sprouting broccoli
400g (14oz) paneer, cut widthways into 8 slabs and scored
150g (5½oz) shiitake mushrooms, stems trimmed, halved if large (alternatively, use button or portobello mushrooms)
8 thick spring onions, cut into 4–5-cm (1½– 2-inch) batons

FOR THE MARINADE
4½ tablespoons soy sauce
2½ tablespoons clear honey
1½ tablespoons toasted sesame oil
1½ tablespoons Shaoxing wine
5 garlic cloves, crushed or finely grated
5-cm (2-inch) piece of fresh root ginger, grated
1 teaspoon white pepper
2 teaspoons lime juice

TO FINISH
1 tablespoon chilli oil
1 teaspoon toasted sesame seeds
Small handful of roughly chopped fresh coriander (optional, but nice)
Squeeze of lime (optional)

1. First make the marinade: whisk together all the ingredients in a bowl until glossy. Transfer to a small pan for 3–4 minutes until reduced enough to coat a spoon. Reserve 1 tablespoon for glazing later.
2. Ensure the paneer slices are roughly the same size as the vegetables and place them all in the marinade. Cover and set aside for up to 30 minutes.
3. Preheat a griddle pan, barbecue or oven grill until medium–hot.
4. Grill the paneer slabs for 2–3 minutes on each side, until golden, lightly charred and warmed through. Grill the broccoli, spring onions and mushrooms alongside them, turning occasionally, until tender and charred at the edges.
5. During the final 1–2 minutes of cooking, brush the paneer and vegetables with the reserved marinade so it caramelises and turns glossy. Keep an eye on it, as the honey and soy can catch quickly over a high heat.
6. Transfer to a platter. Drizzle lightly with chilli oil and sprinkle with toasted sesame seeds. Finish with coriander and a squeeze of lime, if using. Serve immediately on top of sticky rice or with a salad.

SERVES: 4 • PREP TIME: 25–30 MINUTES • COOK TIME: 8–10 MINUTES

Buttery Barbecue Skewers

This barbecue sauce is one for the sceptics – it's not too sweet, firmly savoury and perfect for dipping. Crushed fennel and plenty of butter make it rich, sticky and utterly addictive.

400g (14oz) paneer, cut into large cubes
1 red onion, cut into wedges then layers separated
1 red and 1 yellow bell pepper, deseeded and cut into chunks
Olive oil, for brushing
Pinch of salt
Squeeze of lime or a pinch of flaky salt, to serve (optional)

FOR THE BARBECUE SAUCE
1 tablespoon olive oil
2 garlic cloves, crushed or finely grated
¾ teaspoon fennel seeds, lightly crushed
200g (7oz) tomato passata or crushed tomatoes
2 tablespoons tomato ketchup
1½ tablespoons apple cider vinegar
1½ tablespoons brown sugar or honey
1 teaspoon Dijon mustard
1 tablespoon Worcestershire sauce
1 teaspoon smoked paprika
½ teaspoon ground cumin
½ teaspoon dried oregano
½ teaspoon dried thyme
1 teaspoon onion powder
¼–½ teaspoon chilli powder (optional)
Salt and pepper, to taste
1–2 tablespoons butter

FOR THE LIME YOGURT SLAW
Zest and juice of 1 lime
1 tablespoon olive oil
2 tablespoons thick Greek yogurt
1 teaspoon Dijon mustard
Pinch of salt
Pinch of sugar
140g (5oz) finely shredded white cabbage
1 carrot, grated
1 red onion, finely sliced
Small handful of coriander, chopped
Pepper

1 First make the barbecue sauce: heat the olive oil in a pan over a medium heat. Add the garlic and cook for 30 seconds until fragrant but not coloured. Stir in the fennel seeds and toast briefly.

2 Add the passata, ketchup, vinegar, sugar, mustard and Worcestershire sauce. Stir in the smoked paprika, cumin, oregano, thyme, onion powder and chilli powder, if using. Season with salt and pepper.

3 Simmer gently for 8–10 minutes, stirring occasionally, until thickened and glossy. Remove from the heat and stir in the butter until melted and glossy. Taste and adjust; it should be smoky, tangy and balanced. Allow to cool slightly, then divide the sauce in half – one portion for glazing during cooking, the other for serving.

4 To prepare the slaw, in a large bowl whisk together the lime juice and zest, olive oil, yogurt, mustard, salt, sugar and pepper. Add the cabbage, carrot and red onion and toss until evenly coated. Chill for at least 20 minutes so the flavours settle. Fold through the coriander just before serving.

5 Thread the paneer, red onion and peppers alternately onto skewers. Lightly brush with olive oil and season with a pinch of salt.

6 Preheat a barbecue or griddle pan until medium-hot. Cook the kebabs for 6–8 minutes, turning occasionally, until lightly charred and heated through. During the final 2–3 minutes of cooking, brush generously with the reserved sauce, turning to allow it to caramelize. Watch carefully, as the sugars in the sauce can burn.

7 Arrange the skewers on a platter and serve with the remaining barbecue sauce alongside. Add a squeeze of lime or a pinch of flaky salt just before serving to lift, if you like. Serve immediately with the lime yogurt slaw on the side.

SERVES: 4 • PREP TIME: 15–20 MINUTES (EXCLUDING MARINATION) • COOK TIME: 10–12 MINUTES

Tandoori Paneer Kebabs

No paneer cookbook would be complete without including certain recipes, and tandoori paneer is one of them. It uses a family tandoori marinade created by my father, who is head griller: the result is smoky, aromatic kebabs best grilled with plenty of vegetables.

400g (14oz) paneer, cut into 3-cm (1¼-inch) cubes
1 red onion, cut into wedges then layers separated
1–2 mixed bell peppers, deseeded and cut into large chunks
Melted butter, for brushing (optional)
Fresh coriander, roughly chopped, and a squeeze of lemon, to finish
Coriander Chutney (see page 168) and Pickled Red Onion (see page 111), to serve

FOR THE MARINADE
150g (5½oz) thick Greek yogurt
1 tablespoon lemon juice
1 tablespoon chickpea flour
1 tablespoon mustard oil or neutral oil
1 tablespoon ginger-garlic paste
1 teaspoon Kashmiri (mild) chilli powder
½ teaspoon ground turmeric
1 teaspoon ground coriander
1 teaspoon ground cumin
½ teaspoon carom seeds, lightly crushed
1 teaspoon kasoori methi, crushed
½ teaspoon pepper
1 teaspoon salt

1. First make the marinade: whisk together the yogurt, lemon juice and chickpea flour until smooth. Add the remaining ingredients and mix well – the marinade should be thick enough to coat the paneer generously. Taste and adjust the salt or chilli. Allow to sit for 5–10 minutes to thicken.
2. Add the paneer, onion and peppers to the bowl. Coat gently but thoroughly in the marinade. Cover and marinate in the refrigerator for at least 30 minutes, ideally 2–4 hours.
3. Thread the paneer, onion and peppers alternately onto skewers.
4. If using the grill, preheat it until very hot. Place the skewers on a lined tray and grill for 10–12 minutes, turning once, until lightly charred at the edges.
5. If using a barbecue method, cook the skewers over a medium–high heat for 8–10 minutes, turning regularly, until charred and heated through.
6. Brush the skewers lightly with melted butter in the last minute, if you like.
7. Sprinkle with fresh coriander and a squeeze of lemon juice, to finish. Serve with the chutney and onions.

AUNTY SPECIALS

Aunty Specials

This chapter comes from a place of love. These are family recipes, or variations of them, that have been cooked in kitchens for generations, tweaked slightly by every aunty along the way. They are labours of love, the dishes we turn to when we want to treat someone special.

Communal eating is one of life's greatest pleasures. Whenever I travel somewhere, the first thing I think about is what food I'll be eating. I'll look up cookbooks from the region, eat everything in sight, and ask endless questions. Food tells you so much about a place – its history, its people, its pride.

One of life's richest experiences is seeing someone light up when they talk about their national dish. Everybody has one. It's a joy that doesn't discriminate based on income or background. It's a shared language that anyone can speak.

When my family first came to the UK, food was how they connected with people. It was how they made friends, built community and felt a little less far away from home. Cooking for someone is a way of saying, 'You're welcome here – come and sit with us.'

And sometimes that shared connection is found in the most unexpected places. Chicken tikka masala is widely considered the UK's favourite national dish – a curry born from cultures meeting and blending together. You might think you have nothing in common with the person sitting next to you, but the chances are you both enjoy a good tikka masala. If that alone doesn't tell a celebratory story of cultural exchange, I don't know what does.

These recipes celebrate that spirit. They are the dishes that appear when the table gets bigger, when friends come over, when someone deserves something a little special. They are the ones you make slowly, tasting as you go, adjusting the spices the way your mum or an aunty showed you. They are also the ones you can never quite replicate, even when you follow the recipe exactly. They are celebratory, beautiful and, most importantly, delicious.

SERVES: 4 • PREP TIME: 25 MINUTES, PLUS SOAKING & FERMENTATION • COOK TIME: 25 MINUTES

Paneer Dosa

I've been pretty spoiled by homemade dosa over the years, and watching it get made from scratch still feels like magic, as fermented batter transforms into something crisp and golden. This is my mother's dosa recipe. It's not as intimidating as it might sound, and it is far superior to any store-bought mix (though if you're pressed for time, a good-quality mix will do the job).

200g (7oz) short-grain or idli rice
100g (3½oz) urad dal (black) lentils
½ teaspoon fenugreek seeds
Salt

FOR THE PANEER FILLING
1 tablespoon neutral oil
1 teaspoon mustard seeds
1 teaspoon cumin seeds
8–10 fresh curry leaves
1 onion, finely chopped
1 green chilli, finely chopped (deseed if you want less heat)
3.5-cm (1-inch) piece of fresh root ginger, grated
½ teaspoon turmeric
1 teaspoon ground coriander
400g (14oz) paneer, finely grated or crumbled
Salt, to taste
1 teaspoon garam masala
1 tablespoon chopped fresh coriander
Squeeze of lemon

TO SERVE
South Indian Coconut Chutney (see page 169)
Sambar (see page 170)

1 To make the dosa batter, rinse the rice and soak in water for at least 4 hours. Rinse and soak the urad dal and fenugreek seeds separately for 4 hours. Alternatively, use 650g (1lb 7oz) good-quality ready-made dosa batter and skip ahead to step 4.

2 Drain and blend the urad dal with enough water to form a smooth, fluffy batter. Drain the rice and blend it separately until slightly grainy but smooth.

3 Combine the dal and rice in a large bowl. Mix well, cover and leave in a warm place to ferment for 8–12 hours, until slightly bubbly and airy. Stir in some salt before cooking.

4 To make the paneer filling, heat the oil in a pan over a medium heat. Add the mustard seeds and let them splutter, then add the cumin seeds and curry leaves.

5 Add the onion and cook until soft. Stir in the chilli and ginger and cook for 1 minute. Briefly stir in the turmeric and ground coriander. Add grated paneer and salt to taste. Cook gently for 3–4 minutes, stirring so it absorbs the spices but doesn't dry out. Mix in the garam masala, fresh coriander and a squeeze of lemon.

6 To make the dosa, heat a flat nonstick pan or cast-iron tawa over a medium–high heat. Pour a ladle of the batter into the centre, using the back of the ladle to spread it outwards into a thin circle.

7 Drizzle a little oil or ghee around the edges. Cook until the underside is golden and crisp and the edges lift easily. Do not flip, as dosa cooks only on one side.

8 Spoon a portion of the paneer filling onto one half of the dosa and spread lightly. Fold over and cook for another minute until crisp.

9 Remove and keep hot. Then repeat, making 3 more dosas. Serve hot with the chutney and sambar.

SERVES: 4 • PREP TIME: 15 MINUTES • COOK TIME: 30 MINUTES

Paneer Pav Bhaji

Traditional pav bhaji consists of a mixed vegetable base that's cooked down and mashed slightly, often eaten for breakfast with hot buttered buns, lemon juice and red onion. Adding paneer brings a lovely texture and creates a slightly more balanced dish. Every family has their own way of eating it – we like to dollop the bhaji onto the hot buttered bun and eat it like an open sandwich.

350g (12oz) potatoes, diced
100g (3½oz) cauliflower florets
150g (5½oz) fresh or frozen peas
1 carrot, finely diced
Salt, to taste

FOR THE BHAJI BASE

3 tablespoons butter or ghee, plus extra for finishing
1 tablespoon neutral oil
1 teaspoon cumin seeds
1 large onion, very finely chopped
2–3 tablespoons ginger-garlic paste
2 green chillies, finely chopped or left whole (deseed if you want less heat)
3 large tomatoes, finely chopped or puréed
1 green bell pepper, deseeded and finely chopped
1 tablespoon tomato purée
2–2½ teaspoons Pav Bhaji Masala (see page 164)
¼–1 teaspoon Kashmiri (mild) chilli powder (optional)
¼ teaspoon ground turmeric
Salt, to taste

TO FINISH

400g (14oz) paneer, finely crumbled
1 tablespoon kasoori methi, crushed
1 tablespoon butter
Handful of finely chopped coriander

TO SERVE PAV-BHAJI STYLE

Brioche or burger buns
Butter, for toasting
Finely chopped red onion
Fresh coriander
Lemon wedges

1. Boil the potatoes, cauliflower, peas and carrot in salted water until very soft, then drain and mash the vegetables roughly; the mixture should be broken down but not completely smooth.
2. For the bhaji base, heat the butter or ghee with the oil in a wide pan over a medium heat. Add the cumin seeds and let them splutter. Add the onion and cook for 8–10 minutes, until soft and golden. Stir in the ginger-garlic paste and green chillies. Cook for 1 minute. Add the tomatoes, bell pepper and tomato purée. Cook until thick, glossy and slightly buttery at the edges. Stir in the pav bhaji masala (reserving a pinch for finishing), the chilli powder, turmeric and salt. Cook for 1–2 minutes to bloom the spices.
3. Add the mashed vegetables to the pan and mash again, adding splashes of hot water as needed. Simmer for 10–12 minutes, stirring and mashing occasionally, until rich and scoopable but not dry. It should be thick yet saucy.
4. Fold in the crumbled paneer. Mash lightly, if desired, so some blends in and some remains textured. Simmer for 3–4 minutes to heat through.
5. Stir in the kasoori methi, the butter and chopped coriander. Taste, and adjust the salt and pav bhaji spice if necessary.
6. Cut the buns in half. Heat a flat pan and melt a tablespoon of butter with a pinch of pav bhaji masala. Toast the buns, cut-side down, until golden and buttery.
7. Spoon the pav bhaji into bowls, topped with a knob of butter, some red onion, fresh coriander and the lemon wedges for squeezing over. Serve immediately with the hot buttered buns.

SERVES: 4-6 • PREP TIME: 20 MINUTES (PLUS OVERNIGHT SOAKING) • COOK TIME: 30 MINUTES

Sev Usal with Paneer Tikki

Sev usal is my favourite dish, first made for me by my Madhu Baa (grandma). It is a wonderful feasting dish, and a special, joyful way of feeding those you love.

350g (12oz) cooked white peas (from 200g/7oz dried, soaked overnight; can be substituted with 1 x 400g can chickpeas or butterbeans, drained and rinsed)
2 tablespoons neutral oil
1 teaspoon mustard seeds
1 teaspoon cumin seeds
10 fresh curry leaves
¼ teaspoon asafoetida (optional)
1 onion, finely chopped
2 tablespoons ginger-garlic paste
2 green chillies, finely chopped (deseed if you want less heat)
2 tomatoes, finely chopped
½ teaspoon ground turmeric
1½ teaspoons ground coriander
1 teaspoon ground cumin
1 teaspoon Kashmiri (mild) chilli powder
1–2 teaspoons garam masala
250–350ml (9–12fl oz) hot water
½ teaspoon sugar, for a Gujarati touch (optional)
Salt, to taste

TO FINISH
Squeeze of lemon juice
Small handful chopped coriander

TO SERVE
Paneer tikki, made in advance (see Paneer Tikki Burgers recipe overleaf)
4 tablespoons fine nylon sev (chickpea noodle snack)
4 tablespoons red onion, finely chopped
4 tablespoons tomatoes, chopped
1 teaspoon fresh coriander per portion
Lemon wedges
4 teaspoons Coriander Chutney (page 168, optional)
4 tablespoons Tamarind Chutney (page 168 – a must)

1 If using dried and soaked white beans, pressure-cook with a pinch of salt until soft but holding their shape (15–20 minutes), then drain and reserve some cooking liquid. Alternatively, place in a saucepan with 750–950ml (1½–2 pints) water and a pinch of salt. Simmer gently for 45–60 minutes, until soft but still holding shape. Drain and reserve some cooking liquid. If using canned chickpeas or cannellini beans, no cooking is needed; just set aside after draining and rinsing.

2 Heat the oil in a deep pan. Add the mustard seeds and let them splutter. Add the cumin seeds, curry leaves and asafoetida, if using. Add the onion and cook until soft and lightly golden. Add the ginger-garlic paste and green chillies, cooking for 1 minute. Add the tomatoes and cook until soft and slightly jammy. Stir in the turmeric, ground coriander, ground cumin, chilli powder and garam masala. Cook for 1–2 minutes to release the aromas.

3 Home-cooked peas can now be added to the spice pan along with the measured hot water. Simmer for 10–15 minutes, lightly mashing some of the peas to thicken the gravy. Canned chickpeas or beans can be added with the measured hot water, but should simmer for only 5–7 minutes. Lightly mash for a slightly thicker gravy; you are aiming for a loose, soupy mixture.

4 Add salt and a pinch of sugar (optional). Finish with a squeeze of lemon juice and a sprinkle of fresh coriander.

5 Spoon the hot usal into bowls. Top each bowl generously with the tikki, sev, chopped onion, tomatoes, coriander, lemon wedges and chutneys, if using.

SERVES: 4 • PREP TIME: 25 MINUTES (INCLUDES CHILLING) • COOK TIME: 10 MINUTES

Paneer Tikki Burgers

This is my grandma's recipe for Paneer Tikki: spiced potato patties, seasoned with spices and aromatics, shaped into rounds and pan-fried until crisp. They are incredibly versatile – eat them as they are, tuck them into a sandwich, turn them into burgers or serve alongside Sev Usal (see page 146).

- 300g (10½oz) paneer, finely grated or crumbled
- ½ tablespoon chickpea flour
- 1 large floury potato (about 175g/6oz), boiled and mashed smoothly
- 1–2 green chillies, very finely chopped (deseed if you want less heat)
- 2.5-cm (1-inch) piece of fresh root ginger, finely grated
- 1 garlic clove, crushed or finely grated
- 1 tablespoon finely chopped fresh coriander
- 1 teaspoon ground cumin
- ½ teaspoon ground coriander
- 1 teaspoon garam masala
- ¼–½ teaspoon chilli powder
- ½ teaspoon chaat masala
- 1 teaspoon salt (or to taste)
- ½ teaspoon pepper
- 3 tablespoons sweetcorn, lightly crushed (optional)
- 2–3 tablespoons neutral oil
- 1–2 tablespoons red onion, very finely diced (optional, but recommended)
- 1 tablespoon breadcrumbs (if needed)
- Salt and pepper

TO SERVE

- 4 burger buns
- 1 tablespoon Madhu's Garlic and Chilli Chutney (see page 168)
- 1 tablespoon Coriander Chutney (see page 168)
- 1 tablespoon Pickled Red Onions (see page 111)
- 8 Little Gem lettuce leaves
- Mayonnaise, optional

1 Combine the paneer, chickpea flour and mashed potato in a bowl. Add all the remaining ingredients, apart from the breadcrumbs and oil. Mix gently until just combined, being careful not to overwork. The mixture should hold together when pressed. If it feels too soft or sticky, mix in 1 tablespoon of breadcrumbs. Add more chickpea flour only if necessary.

2 Divide the mixture into 4 equal portions and shape into flat rounds around 2.5-cm (1-inch) deep. Place on a tray and chill for 20–30 minutes to help the patties firm up and hold their shape.

3 Heat the oil in a wide, heavy-based frying pan over a medium heat and tilt so it lightly coats the pan. Once hot, add the patties. Cook for 3–4 minutes per side until deep golden and crisp. Avoid moving them too early so a crust can form. Flip carefully using a spatula and cook the second side until evenly browned. Drain briefly on kitchen paper.

4 Lightly toast the burger buns. Spread the garlic and chilli chutney on the base of each bun and the coriander chutney on the top half, followed by mayo, if using. Place a layer of lettuce on the base, followed by the hot paneer tikki. Spoon over a little of the pickled red onion, then sit the other bun half on top. Serve immediately while the tikki is crisp.

PREP TIME: 5 MINUTES • COOK TIME: 10 MINUTES

The Dhungar Method

If you've never tried - or even heard of - the dhungar method of smoking food, this is your moment. It's a simple technique used across Indian cooking to add a deep, smoky flavour, no barbecue required.

Paneer is perfect for this technique- soft and milky, it absorbs the smoke beautifully while still holding its texture. It feels a little theatrical (there's hot charcoal involved), but it is surprisingly easy - a brilliant way to elevate a dish without firing up the barbecue. You can also use it, as we have overleaf, in curry. It's ideal in the Dal to bring a smoky edge to the rich creaminess.

1–2 pieces of charcoal
1 teaspoon ghee or oil (mustard oil is good for imparting a strong flavour)
Food for smoking, such as cooked paneer or curry

1. Heat the pieces of charcoal over a gas flame using metal tongs until red hot and lightly ashed. This takes about 5–6 minutes.
2. Place your cooked paneer or curry in a deep pot or bowl with a tight-fitting lid, such as a deep saucepan or casserole dish. You can even put the dish holding the food into the pan, too.
3. Set a small steel bowl or a cup made from aluminium foil in the centre of the pan (see photo overleaf).
4. Carefully place the hot charcoal into the bowl using tongs.
5. Immediately pour the ghee or oil over the charcoal. It will begin smoking straight away.
6. Quickly cover the pan with a lid to trap the smoke.
7. Leave to smoke for 2–5 minutes for a light flavour, or up to 10 minutes for something more intense.
8. Remove the lid and carefully lift out the charcoal bowl. Stir the paneer or curry gently and serve.

SERVES: 4 AS A MAIN, 8 AS A SIDE • PREP TIME: 12 HOURS (INCLUDING SOAKING) • COOK TIME: 5 HOURS

5-hour Black Dal

I can confidently say that this is one of the best dals you will ever eat. Urad beans (black lentils) are what give black dal its signature silky creamy texture. They can handle a lot of flavour, so the aromatics feature large here and develop over time. The result is deeply rich and satisfying, and more than enough to be enjoyed on its own. It is worth every minute spent on it.

200g (7oz) urad dal (whole black lentils)
50g (1¾oz) red kidney beans
4 tablespoons ghee
2 bay leaves
8 green cardamoms
5 peppercorns
1 large cinnamon stick
6 cloves
2 onions, finely chopped
3 tablespoons ginger-garlic paste
200g (7oz) tomato purée
1–2 teaspoons salt to taste
1½ teaspoons Kashmiri (mild) red chilli powder, to taste
1 teaspoon garam masala
875ml (31fl oz) hot water
1–2 teaspoons jaggery or sugar, to taste (optional)
1 tablespoon kasoori methi, crushed (optional)
4–6 tablespoons double cream or cashew cream, plus extra for garnish
Butter

TO SERVE (OPTIONAL)
Garlic-ginger tadka (page 162)
Handful of coriander, chopped
Pickled Red Onions (see page 111)
Steamed rice
Naans
Kachumber Salad (see page 166)

1 Rinse the urad dal and red kidney beans thoroughly, rubbing them together. Repeat 2–3 times. Cover with plenty of water and leave to soak overnight. Drain and rinse before use.

2 To pressure-cook the lentils and beans, add 500ml (18fl oz) of the hot water and cook for 25–30 minutes over a medium heat. Alternatively, place in a saucepan with the 500ml (18fl oz) water and bring to the boil on the hob. Simmer gently for 60–75 minutes until very soft and mashable.

3 When ready, heat the ghee in a heavy-based pan. Add the bay leaves, cardamoms, peppercorns, cinnamon stick and cloves; sizzle for 1 minute. Add the onions and sauté for 7 minutes, until golden.

4 Stir in ginger-garlic paste then cook for 1 minute until aromatic. Add the tomato purée and cook for 3–4 minutes.

5 Add salt, chilli powder and garam masala then sauté for 4–5 minutes until the masala thickens.

6 Slightly mash the cooked bean mixture and add to the spice pan. Stir in 250ml (9fl oz) of the remaining hot water and mix well. Cook over a low heat until thick, stirring often to prevent sticking.

7 After 60 minutes, add another 125ml (4fl oz) hot water. Continue simmering for 1½ hours, or up to 8 for a richer flavour, until the dal is very thick. If you want to add a smoky flavour using the Dhungar Method (see page 149), you can do so at this point.

8 Stir the crushed kasoori methi into the dal, then pour in double cream or cashew cream and cook for 6–8 minutes, until thick and creamy.

9 Taste and add salt, sugar or jaggery and more garam masala, if necessary. Add a little butter for extra richness.

10 Garnish with the garlic-ginger tadka, fresh coriander and pickled red onions as desired. Serve hot with rice, naans and a kachumber salad. This makes a great side dish for other curries within this chapter.

SERVES: 4 • PREP TIME: 2–3 HOURS (INCLUDING DOUGH RESTING) • COOK TIME: 1 HOUR

Paneer Chole Bhatura

One of my favourite dishes, this combines delicious chickpeas with fluffy, paneer-stuffed bread.

250g (9oz) plain flour
2 tablespoons semolina (optional)
1 teaspoon sugar and ½ teaspoon salt
½ teaspoon baking powder
½ teaspoon bicarbonate of soda
3 tablespoons yogurt
2 tablespoons oil, plus extra for deep frying
125ml (4fl oz) warm water as needed

FOR THE FILLING
200g (7oz) paneer, very finely grated
1 teaspoon garam masala
1 green chilli, finely chopped (deseed if you want less heat)
½ teaspoon salt
1 handful of coriander, chopped

FOR THE CHOLE (CHICKPEA CURRY)
2 tablespoons oil
1 bay leaf and 4 cloves
1 black cardamom and 3 green cardamom pods
1–2 teaspoons cumin seeds
1 large onion, finely chopped
3 tablespoons ginger-garlic paste
2 tomatoes, finely chopped
1 tablespoon tomato purée
1½ teaspoons ground coriander
1 teaspoon ground cumin
1 teaspoon Kashmiri (mild) chilli powder
½ teaspoon ground turmeric
800g cooked chickpeas, drained
1 teaspoon chole or garam masala
1 teaspoon amchur or lemon juice
Salt, to taste
Fresh coriander, to garnish
1 tablespoon ghee, to finish (optional)

1 To make the bhatura dough, combine the flour, semolina, sugar, salt, baking powder and bicarbonate of soda in a large bowl. Add the yogurt and oil and mix with your fingers until crumbly. Gradually add the warm water, a little at a time, kneading into a soft, smooth dough. It should be softer than rotli dough but not sticky. Cover and rest in a warm place for 1–2 hours.

2 Prepare the paneer filling in a bowl, mixing the finely grated paneer with garam masala, green chilli, salt and coriander. Mix gently until evenly combined – the filling should be dry and crumbly. Cover and set aside.

3 To make the chole, heat the oil in a heavy-based pan over a medium heat. Add the bay leaf, cloves, cardamom pods and cumin seeds; sizzle until fragrant. Add the onion and cook slowly until golden, then stir in the ginger-garlic paste and cook for 1–2 minutes, until aromatic. Add the tomatoes and tomato purée and cook until thick, glossy and the oil begins to separate. Stir in the coriander, cumin, chilli powder and turmeric. Allow to cook for 1–2 minutes before adding the chickpeas with around 250ml (9fl oz) hot water. Simmer gently for 20–25 minutes, partially covered, then lightly mash some chickpeas against the side of the pan to thicken the gravy. Stir in the chole masala, amchur and salt to taste. Add a splash of hot water if needed – the gravy should be thick and coating. Finish with fresh coriander and optional ghee. Set aside and keep warm.

4 Divide the rested dough into 4 equal balls. Flatten one slightly in your palm. Place 2–3 tablespoons of paneer filling in the centre. Bring up the edges and pinch tightly along the top. Gently flatten and roll into a medium disc, 12–15cm (5–6 inches) wide. Roll carefully to prevent the filling from breaking through. Repeat with the remaining dough.

5 Heat a 5-cm (2-inch) depth of oil in a deep pan to 180°C (350°F). Slide one bhatura carefully into hot oil. Gently press down with a slotted spoon to encourage puffing. Fry until golden on one side, then flip and fry until evenly golden on the other side. Remove and drain briefly on kitchen paper. Repeat with the remaining bhatura.

6 Serve the puffed paneer bhatura with the hot chole.

SERVES: 4–6 • PREP TIME: 25–30 MINUTES • COOK TIME: 50 MINUTES

Paneer Pasanda

Layering an aromatic saffron and yogurt curry base with chutney and cashew-stuffed paneer, dishes don't get more celebratory than a Pasanda.

5 tablespoons neutral oil
4 onions, finely chopped
Pinch of salt
9-cm (3-inch) fresh root ginger, roughly chopped
10 garlic cloves, crushed
4–5 tomatoes, diced
75g (2¾oz) cashews, soaked
250g (9oz) plain yogurt
3 tablespoons butter
2 bay leaves
2 strands of mace (optional)
1 cinnamon stick
9 cloves and 9 green cardamom pods
2 black cardamom pods (optional)
2 green chillies, slit and deseeded
1½ teaspoons Kashmiri (mild) chilli powder
2 teaspoons garam masala
1¾–2 teaspoons salt, to taste
1 teaspoon sugar (optional)
½ teaspoon ground black pepper
1 tablespoon kasoori methi, crushed
¼ teaspoon nutmeg, freshly grated
2 pinches of saffron, bloomed in 1 tablespoon cold water (optional)
600g (1lb 5oz) paneer, cut into 8 large rectangles
1 extra tablespoon paneer, finely crumbled (if leftover from slices)
3½ tablespoons finely chopped cashews, pistachios or almonds
3 tablespoons Coriander Chutney (see page 168)
½ teaspoon garam masala
½ teaspoon amchur or chaat masala
2 teaspoons ghee

1. Heat the oil in a large, heavy-bottomed pan over a medium heat. Fry the onions and a pinch of salt for 20 minutes, stirring often, until soft and golden. This step is essential to building flavour – don't rush it. Add the ginger and garlic and cook over a low heat for 5–7 minutes, until the onions are caramelized. Allow to cool slightly.

2. Transfer the onion mixture to a blender or food processor. Add the tomatoes, soaked cashews and yogurt and blend to a very smooth paste.

3. In the empty pan, melt the butter over a low heat. Add the bay leaves, mace, cinnamon stick, cloves, cardamom pods and green chillies. Sauté gently for 1 minute, until fragrant. Stir in the chilli powder and garam masala, then pour in the blended onion mixture. Partially cover and cook over a low–medium heat for 8–10 minutes, stirring often until the mixture thickens and the fat begins to separate.

4. Over a low heat, gradually add 700ml (1¼ pints) hot water, stirring to create a creamy gravy. Cover and simmer for 20 minutes, stirring occasionally, until rich and glossy. Season with salt, sugar, if using, black pepper, kasoori methi, nutmeg and saffron. Taste and adjust seasoning. Keep warm.

5. To prepare the filling, combine the crumbled paneer, chopped nuts, chutney, garam masala and amchur in a bowl. Mix gently until moist but firm.

6. Cut a horizontal slit in one side of each paneer rectangle, taking care not to cut all the way through, so the base it still hinged. Stuff the slit with the filling and press gently to close and keep the filling.

7. Heat the ghee in a wide pan over a medium heat. Fry the stuffed paneer in batches, turning carefully, until golden and lightly crisp on both sides. Remove and keep warm. Just before serving, place the fried paneer sandwiches in the hot gravy, spooning it over each one, and simmer for 2–3 minutes, allowing the paneer to absorb the flavours without becoming too soft.

8. Serve hot with basmati rice or naans and a side of Red Onion Salad (see page 167), if liked.

SERVES: 4 • PREP TIME: 40 MINUTES • COOK TIME: 30 MINUTES

Malai Paneer Kofta

Give meatballs the day off and make these melt-in-the-mouth Kofta, with an irresistible balance of sweet and salty. Simmered in a creamy tomato sauce, this is a great family-friendly dish.

200g (7oz) paneer, finely grated or very finely crumbled
150g (5½oz) potato, peeled, boiled, and mashed
1 tablespoon cornflour
1 tablespoon milk powder (optional)
1 teaspoon chaat masala (optional)
2 tablespoons finely chopped coriander
2 tablespoons raisins
Neutral oil, for frying
Salt, to taste

FOR THE GRAVY
10 cashews, soaked for 15 minutes in 2 tablespoons of hot water
10 almonds, or 6–8 walnuts, soaked
3 tomatoes, roughly chopped
3 tablespoons ghee or butter
2 bay leaves
1 cinnamon stick
1 star anise
4 cardamom pods
3 cloves
2 onions, very finely chopped
1 tablespoon ginger-garlic paste
¼ teaspoon ground turmeric
½ teaspoon white pepper
¼ teaspoon freshly grated nutmeg
½ teaspoon sugar
100g (3½oz) yogurt, whisked
100ml (3½fl oz) milk
1 teaspoon garam masala
1 teaspoon kasoori methi (optional)

1 Place the grated paneer and potato in a wide bowl. Mix with your fingertips until just combined, then add the cornflour, milk powder, chaat masala, coriander, raisins and salt. Mix lightly until the mixture comes together and is able to hold its shape. If it feels slightly sticky, chill for 15–20 minutes. Roll into 10–12 evenly sized balls.

2 Heat a layer of the oil in a shallow pan over a medium heat. Add the kofta carefully, taking care not to overcrowd, and cook, turning gently, until golden on all sides. Alternatively, air-fry at 180°C (350°F) for 20 minutes. Remove with a slotted spoon and drain on kitchen paper. Set aside.

3 Now start the gravy: blitz the soaked cashews and almonds in a blender or food processor with a splash of water until completely smooth. Add the tomatoes and blend again until silky, uniform and smooth.

4 Heat the ghee in a heavy-based pan over a medium–low heat. Add the bay leaves, cinnamon stick, star anise, cardamom and cloves, allowing them to release their aroma without letting them darken. Add the onions and cook slowly for 10–15 minutes until softened and lightly golden. Stir in the ginger-garlic paste and cook until the raw smell disappears. Add the tomato and nut paste and cook for 10 minutes, until the fat begins to separate. Stir in the turmeric, white pepper, nutmeg, sugar and some salt.

5 Once thickened, lower the heat and add the prepared nut paste, cooking gently for 3–4 minutes while stirring continuously. Gradually add the whisked yogurt, stirring constantly to prevent it from splitting. Pour in the milk and simmer for 5–8 minutes, until the gravy is thick and glossy. The oils should begin to slightly separate, indicating the spices have cooked out. Stir in the garam masala and crushed kasoori methi, if using.

6 Add the kofta to the gravy just before serving and simmer for 2–3 minutes. Avoid boiling, as the kofta will soften too much. Set aside to rest for about 5 minutes before serving so the kofta can absorb the flavours of the sauce.

SERVES: 4–6 • PREP TIME: 25 MINUTES (PLUS AT LEAST 4 HOURS CHILLING) • COOK TIME: 30 MINUTES

Ras Malai

Paneer isn't just for savoury dishes! Ras malai is a Bengali dessert of soft paneer dumplings in a sweet, fragrant milky sauce. It really is crucial to use the right paneer here; if it's not soft enough, it won't turn into a dough or hold together in the syrup. Our All the Aunties plain paneer works beautifully, or you could make your own! (see page 11.)

400g (14oz) All the Aunties plain paneer, softened in hot water for 10–15 minutes
¼ teaspoon bicarbonate of soda
1 tablespoon icing sugar

FOR THE SYRUP
750ml (1½ pints) water
150g (5oz) sugar
1 teaspoon vanilla extract
Pinch of salt

FOR THE MILK MIXTURE/MALAI
480ml (17fl oz) full-fat milk
240g (8½fl oz) condensed milk
4 cardamom pods, lightly crushed
Pinch of saffron
½ teaspoon rose water or kewra water (optional, but lovely)

TO FINISH
Crushed pistachios or pistachio butter
Rose petals

1. Grate or crumble the paneer into a bowl then mix in the bicarbonate of soda and icing sugar. Knead firmly with the heel of your hand for 10–15 minutes, until it is smooth, slightly creamy and holds together without cracking. Continue kneading if cracks appear when shaping.

2. Divide the dough into 8–10 equal pieces and roll each into a ball. Gently flatten into discs about 4–5cm (1½–2 inches) wide. Ensure the discs are completely smooth to prevent breakage.

3. To make the syrup, combine the ingredients in a wide, deep pan. Bring to a gentle rolling boil, then reduce to a steady simmer.

4. Carefully slide the paneer discs into the simmering syrup without overcrowding (work in batches if necessary). Cook uncovered on medium heat for 5–10 minutes. They will puff slightly and soften. Remove carefully with a slotted spoon and set aside to cool slightly in the fridge.

5. To prepare the malai, combine the milks in a separate saucepan, then add the cardamom and saffron. Heat gently over a low–medium heat, stirring occasionally, for about 8–10 minutes, until slightly thickened and fragrant. Remove from the heat and stir in rose or kewra water, if using. Allow to cool slightly, then remove the cardamom pods.

6. To assemble, gently press each cooked paneer disc between your palms to remove excess syrup – do not squeeze firmly or the discs may break. Place them in the warm milk mixture, ensuring they are fully submerged. Allow to cool completely, then refrigerate for at least 2 hours, preferably overnight.

7. Spoon plenty of malai over each serving (allow 2–3 discs per person). Garnish with crushed pistachios, or a small spoon of pistachio butter, and rose petals. Serve chilled.

Aunty says not to panic if some crumbles start to dissipate in the syrup - this is normal!

STORE-CUPBOARD ESSENTIALS

Cooking quickly, easily and with big flavour isn't about having hundreds of ingredients – it's about having the right ones. Every family will have their own version of a well-stocked kitchen, but this is ours.

THE ANATOMY OF A DISH

Think of the components of a recipe as you would a capsule wardrobe:

- Oils and fats are your foundation.
- Spices bring personality and flavour.
- Aromatics are your foundation builders.
- Vegetables give the dish its substance.
- Protein is the statement piece.
- Carbohydrates bring structure and comfort.
- Herbs, sauces, chutneys and fresh elements are the finishing touches.

Like a good outfit, building a good dish is all about layering.

Start with fat – and don't be shy (I have honestly never seen an Aunty measure oil with a teaspoon). Add whole spices and let them toast, releasing their flavour into the oil. Follow with your aromatics: onion, garlic, ginger. Season as you go; salt is not a final step, it is part of the process. Then come your vegetables and protein.

At this point, think about your carbohydrates – rice, rotli, potatoes or grains – the element that gives the dish structure and makes it a complete meal. Whether they're cooked alongside or served underneath, they carry everything else and bring it together.

Balance it all with a little acid and, if needed, a touch of sugar. Finish with something fresh – herbs, chutney or yogurt – to lift it all.

If you start doing only two things, make them this: bloom your spices in hot fat and season as you go. These two habits alone will transform your cooking.

Remember, 'spice' doesn't always mean heat. It can be as simple as black pepper or cumin seeds. Think boiled potatoes. Now think boiled potatoes tossed with a three-finger pinch of salt and cumin seeds sizzled in olive oil. It's a completely different dish.

The final flourish is just as important. Many dishes in this book are finished with chutneys, pickles, herby sauces or yogurt. That last hit of brightness or richness can turn something good into something *really* good. It might be as simple as stirring lemon juice and zest into yogurt, or mixing chopped herbs with garlic and olive oil.

Tadkas (see pages 162–163) are another powerful way to layer flavour at the end – hot oil infused with spices and aromatics, poured over a finished dish. They are a staple in Indian homes for a reason. If you want to get ahead, make a batch to keep on hand, or go all in with the Masala Chilli Crisp (see page 171) – it goes on everything.

WHAT SHOULD YOU HAVE IN YOUR STORE CUPBOARD?

Think of this as a mix-and-match system. Each category brings something different to the dish, and you don't need everything – just enough to build flavour in layers. Once you have a few staples from each, you can cook almost everything without following a recipe.

Oils and fats: your foundation

- Neutral cooking oil (such as vegetable, sunflower or grapeseed oil)
- Ghee
- Coconut oil (for South Indian cooking)
- Mustard oil (for Bengali cuisine)

Spices: flavour builders

- Ground cumin, coriander, turmeric
- Red chilli powder, chilli flakes
- Garam masala
- Whole cumin seeds, mustard seeds
- Cardamom pods, cloves, cinnamon sticks
- Fennel seeds
- Curry leaves, bay leaves
- Kasoori methi (essential for finishing)
- Smoked paprika, black pepper
- Black cardamom (for smokiness)
- White sesame seeds

Aromatics: foundation builders

- Onions and shallots
- Garlic and ginger

Vegetables: depth and body

- Tomatoes (canned or fresh)
- Tomato purée
- Frozen peas
- Aubergine, cauliflower, broccoli, courgette (meaty, versatile veg)

Protein: the statement piece

- Beans and pulses
- Paneer (freezes well)
- Tofu or tempeh
- Chicken

Carbohydrates: for structure

- Rice, potatoes
- Paratha, rotli, naan (made with various flours: chickpea, wholewheat, rice)
- Sourdough bread
- Grains: pearl barley, bulgur, couscous
- Lentils and beans: red lentils, chickpeas, kidney beans, black-eyed beans

Herbs and fresh elements: to lift

- Coriander, dill, parsley, mint, basil
- Lemons and limes
- Fresh chillies

Sauces, pastes and umami boosters: shortcuts to depth

- Garlic-chilli paste
- Miso, gochujang, harissa, pesto
- Soy sauce, sesame oil

Chutneys and finishing extras: the final flourish

- Coriander, garlic or chilli chutneys
- Raita
- Pickles
- Tadkas

With these ingredients in your kitchen, you don't need a recipe. It's just a way of thinking. Simply pick, mix and layer. This is how Aunties cook: by instinct, by layering, by knowing how to make something out of anything.

Combine a fat with an aromatic, a spice, a vegetable, a protein and add something sharp at the end – and then you have dinner. Every time.

Tadkas

Tadkas are quite possibly the world's greatest flavour boosters – a proper secret weapon. Hot fat, whole spices and aromatics crackle away to become a final flavour hit over dals, rice, vegetables or even salads. These are the classics I always come back to. Use them to finish a dish or serve alongside. A good tadka can totally transform a meal from okay to amazing.

Making a tadka is so nostalgic for me – as a child, the smell and the sound drifting from the kitchen were sure markers that dinner was about to be ready, so I love making them. Plus it really does take just two minutes.

You can find recipes for a Brown Butter Tadka alongside the Paneer Butter Masala on page 64; a Curry Leaf & Fennel Tadka alongside the Keralan-inspired Beetroot & Coconut Curry on page 69; and the Dal Tadka within the Dal recipe on page 76.

CURRY LEAF & MUSTARD SEED TADKA

Best for: dals, yogurt, simple veg

1 tablespoon neutral oil or ghee
½ teaspoon mustard seeds
½ teaspoon urad dal (optional)
10–12 curry leaves
Pinch of asafoetida (optional)
1 tablespoon roughly chopped cashew nuts (optional)

Heat the oil or ghee in a small pan over a medium heat until shimmering.

Add the mustard seeds and let them pop.

Add the urad dal and cashews, if using, and fry for 30–60 seconds, stirring, until lightly golden.

Add the curry leaves (stand back – they will splutter) and asafoetida, and fry for 30–60 seconds, until fragrant. Remove from the heat and pour immediately over the dish.

GARLIC-GINGER TADKA

Best for: everyday essential

2 tablespoons neutral oil or ghee
4 garlic cloves, finely sliced
1 tablespoon julienned or finely chopped fresh root ginger

Heat the oil or ghee in a small pan over a medium heat until shimmering.

Add the garlic and cook for 30–40 seconds, stirring, until lightly golden at the edges.

Add the ginger and fry for 30–60 seconds, until fragrant.

Remove from the heat and pour immediately over the dish.

GARLIC-CHILLI TADKA

Best for: punchy finishes, eggs, greens, noodles

1 tablespoon neutral oil or ghee
4 garlic cloves, thinly sliced
2 red or green chillies, finely sliced (deseed if you want less heat)
½ teaspoon salt

Heat the oil or ghee in a small pan over a medium heat until shimmering.

Add the garlic and cook for 30–60 seconds, stirring, until lightly golden at the edges.

Add the chillies and fry for a 30–60 seconds, until fragrant.

Remove from the heat, stir in the salt and pour immediately over your dish.

CHILLI OIL TADKA

Best for: eggs, paneer, noodles, anything needing a kick

3 tablespoons neutral oil
2 garlic cloves, thinly sliced
1 teaspoon chilli flakes
1 teaspoon sesame seeds
1 teaspoon soy sauce
Pinch of sugar
Pinch of salt

Heat the oil in a small pan over a medium heat until shimmering but not smoking.

Add the garlic and cook for 30–60 seconds, stirring, until lightly golden.

Remove the pan from the heat and immediately stir in the chilli flakes and sesame seeds. Let them sizzle gently in the hot oil for a few seconds.

Add the sugar and salt, then leave to bloom for 30 seconds, before spooning over your dish.

ONION–TOMATO TADKA (FOR DAL)

Best for: hearty dals, when you want body

6 tablespoons neutral oil
1 teaspoon cumin seeds
4 onions, finely chopped
1 tablespoon ginger-garlic paste
2 teaspoons red chilli powder
1 teaspoon ground turmeric
3 teaspoons ground coriander
3–4 medium tomatoes, puréed
Salt

Heat the oil in a pan over a medium heat until shimmering. Add the cumin seeds and let them sizzle for a few seconds, until fragrant.

Add the onions and cook for 10–15 minutes, stirring occasionally, until deeply golden and caramelized.

Stir in the ginger-garlic paste and cook for 1–2 minutes.

Add the chilli powder, turmeric and coriander and cook for 20–30 seconds, stirring, until aromatic.

Add the purée and salt, and cook for 8–10 minutes, stirring occasionally, until thickened and the oil begins to separate at the edges.

Spoon over hot dal and simmer together for a few minutes to allow the flavours to meld.

Masalas (spice mixes)

Much to my grandma's dismay, I don't always make my own masalas. Life is too busy for that. But when I do, it's genuinely transformative, and far easier than you think. They last longer, cost less and taste infinitely better.

Some blends in this book, such as chole masala or biryani masala, are a little niche. You can swap in garam masala, but it won't be quite the same. If you've got a well-stocked cupboard, you'll likely have everything you need. If not, they're easy to find in supermarkets or at your local Asian grocer… either way, it's worth it.

Every family has their own garam masala. My grandma's used over 20 spices. This version here is inspired by hers, but the joy of making your own is that you can tweak it entirely to your taste. Hate cloves? Then simply leave them out.

See the method for all masalas in the final paragraph opposite.

PAV BHAJI MASALA

MAKES 70G (2½OZ)

WHOLE SPICES

2 tablespoons coriander seeds
2 teaspoons cumin seeds
1 teaspoon fennel seeds
1 teaspoon black peppercorns
4–5 cloves
1 black cardamom or 2 green cardamom pods
1 small piece of cinnamon or ½ teaspoon ground cinnamon
2 dried red chillies, or 1 teaspoon chilli flakes

GROUND SPICES (ADD AFTER GRINDING)

1 teaspoon turmeric
1½ teaspoons amchur (dry mango powder)
1 teaspoon ground ginger or ½ teaspoon finely chopped fresh root ginger
½ teaspoon salt (optional)

OPTIONAL (ADD WITH WHOLE SPICES)

½ teaspoon caraway or extra cumin seeds
1 small piece of star anise
1 bay leaf

CHOLE MASALA

MAKES 50G (1¾OZ)

2 tablespoons coriander seeds
1 tablespoon cumin seeds
1 teaspoon black peppercorns
4–5 cloves
2–3 green cardamom pods
1 black cardamom pod (optional)
1 small cinnamon stick
1 bay leaf
1–2 dried red chillies
1 teaspoon fennel seeds
½ teaspoon ajwain (carom) seeds (optional)

ADD AFTER ROASTING (DON'T ROAST THESE):
1 teaspoon amchur (dry mango powder)
½ teaspoon ground turmeric
½–1 teaspoon salt (optional)

BIRYANI MASALA

MAKES 70G (2½OZ)

WHOLE SPICES (TO ROAST AND GRIND)
2 tablespoons coriander seeds
2 tablespoons cumin seeds
1 tablespoon fennel seeds
1 tablespoon black peppercorns
10 green cardamom pods
3 black cardamom pods
1½ teaspoons cloves
2–3 small cinnamon sticks
2 star anise
2 blades of mace
4–5 bay leaves

POWDERED OR GRATED SPICES (ADD AFTER GRINDING)
1–2 teaspoons chilli powder
½ teaspoon ground turmeric
1 teaspoon ground ginger
1 teaspoon garlic powder
½ whole nutmeg, grated

GARAM MASALA

MAKES 40G (1½OZ)

2 tablespoons coriander seeds
1 tablespoon cumin seeds
1½ tablespoons black peppercorns
5-cm (2-inch) cinnamon stick
1 tablespoon cloves
1 tablespoon fennel seeds
8–10 green cardamom pods
1 large star anise
2 bay leaves

Method for all masalas

Place the whole spices (including optional ones if using) in a dry pan over a low–medium heat. Roast for 3–5 minutes, stirring continuously until fragrant, but don't let them darken or burn.

Remove from the pan and set aside to cool completely. If there are any spices to be grated (nutmeg, cinnamon stick), do this before grinding. Grind the cooked spices using a spice grinder or mortar and pestle until fine.

Stir in any ground spices (such as turmeric, amchur, chilli powder, ginger, garlic) and salt and mix thoroughly.

Transfer to an airtight container and keep in a cool, dark place. Best used within 3–4 months for peak aroma.

Side Salads

There are a few salads that will feature in most Indian households - something crunchy, fresh and tangy to offset the main meal. These are the kind of side salads that go with everything. Spoon them out alongside curries, tuck them into wraps, or pile them onto plates. They bring balance, brightness and texture.

KACHUMBER SALAD

SERVES: 4 • PREP TIME: 10 MINUTES

2 tomatoes, finely chopped (seeds removed if watery)
1 small cucumber, finely chopped (seeds removed if watery)
1 small red onion, very finely chopped
1 green chilli, very finely chopped and deseeded if you want less heat (optional)
½ teaspoon salt, or to taste
½ teaspoon ground cumin
2 tablespoons lemon juice
2 tablespoons finely chopped coriander
Pinch of black pepper

Place the tomatoes, cucumber and red onion in a bowl. Add the green chilli, if using. Sprinkle over the salt and ground cumin, add the lemon juice and toss gently to combine.

Fold through the chopped coriander and a pinch of black pepper. Taste and adjust salt or lemon juice as needed.

PORIYAL

SERVES: 4 • PREP TIME: 10–15 MINUTES
COOK TIME: 7–10 MINUTES

2 tablespoons neutral oil
1 teaspoon mustard seeds
2 dried red chillies, broken into pieces
450g (1lb) green beans, broccoli or snap peas, trimmed and cut into bite-sized pieces (about 2cm/1inch)
¼ teaspoon asafoetida
10 curry leaves (use fresh if available)
1 teaspoon salt
20g (¾ oz) unsweetened desiccated coconut

FOR THE PODI GARNISH (OPTIONAL)
I teaspoon chana/urad dal (black lentils)
½ tablespoon cumin seeds
½ tablespoon coriander seeds
1 teaspoon fennel seeds
1 red chilli
Salt

For the podi garnish, if making, dry-roast the chana dal in a small pan over a medium heat until lightly golden. Add the cumin and coriander seeds, the fennel seeds and red chilli, and roast briefly until fragrant. Leave to cool.

Grind the podi to a coarse powder, adding a touch of salt.

To make the poriyal, heat the oil in a wide pan over a medium–high heat. When hot, add the mustard seeds and allow them to pop.

Add the dried red chillies and cook for 1–2 minutes, until the dal turns light golden. Add the asafoetida and curry leaves and stir briefly until fragrant.

Add the green vegetables and salt. Cook, partially covered, for 5–7 minutes, stirring occasionally, until tender but still bright and lightly crisp.

Stir in the desiccated coconut and cook for 1 minute to warm through. Remove from heat. Sprinkle the podi garnish (if using) over the poriyal just before serving.

TOMATO SALAD

SERVES: 4 • PREP TIME: 10 MINUTES

3–4 ripe tomatoes, cut into large chunks
1 small red onion, thinly sliced
2 tablespoons roughly chopped fresh coriander
1 mild green chilli, finely chopped
½–1 teaspoon ground cumin
1–2 tablespoons lemon or lime juice, to taste
Salt, to taste
1 tablespoon olive oil or avocado oil

In a large bowl, combine the tomatoes, red onion, coriander and green chilli.

Season with salt, cumin and 1 tablespoon of the citrus juice and some salt. Gently toss to combine, taking care not to break up the tomatoes.

Taste and adjust with more citrus juice or salt, as needed.

Drizzle over the oil and lightly toss.

Serve immediately alongside rich or spiced dishes, as the fresh acidity and light juices are designed to cut through heavier flavours.

ONION (PYAZ) SALAD

SERVES: 6–8 • PREP TIME: 10 MINUTES

2 red onions, thinly sliced into rings and separated
2 tablespoons finely chopped fresh coriander
½ teaspoon chaat masala or ground cumin
¼ teaspoon chilli powder (optional)
1–2 tablespoons lemon or lime juice, to taste
Salt, to taste

Place the sliced onions in a bowl of cold water and soak for 5–10 minutes, then drain well. This mellows their sharpness while keeping them crisp.

Transfer to a bowl and add the coriander. Season with salt, the chaat masala, chilli powder, if using, and 1 tablespoon of citrus juice.

Toss gently with your hands until evenly coated, keeping the onion rings intact. Taste and adjust with more citrus juice or salt, as needed.

Serve immediately as an accompaniment to curries or dals, or as a barbecue dish.

EASY RAITA

SERVES: 4–6 • PREP TIME: 10 MINUTES
COOK TIME: 5 MINUTES

1 cucumber, seeds removed and grated
500g (1lb 2oz) yogurt
½ teaspoon ground cumin
¼ teaspoon salt

FOR THE TEMPERING

1 tablespoon neutral oil
½ teaspoon mustard seeds
5 curry leaves
1 green chilli, slit lengthways and deseeded if you want less heat (optional)
¼ teaspoon asafoetida (optional)

Grate the cucumber into a clean cloth and gently squeeze out the excess liquid. Set aside.

In a bowl, whisk the yogurt until smooth and creamy.

Add the grated cucumber, cumin and salt to the yogurt, then mix well and set aside.

Heat the oil in a small pan over a medium heat. Add the mustard seeds and let them crackle, then add the curry leaves, green chilli and asafoetida, if using. Fry for 20–30 seconds, until fragrant.

Pour the hot tempering over the yogurt mixture and stir gently to combine.

Chill briefly or serve at room temperature.

Chutneys

These are the chutneys I always have to hand – those that tend to end up on everything. They are proper flavour builders... spoon them over, stir them through, or enjoy them straight from the jar. Most of these are family recipes that feature across all sorts of dishes in this book. They freeze well, but in reality rarely last long enough for that.

CORIANDER CHUTNEY

SERVES: 6–8 • PREP TIME: 10 MINUTES

60g coriander, finely chopped
1 green chilli, roughly chopped (deseed if you want less heat)
1 garlic clove, roughly chopped
2.5-cm (1-inch) piece of fresh root ginger, finely chopped
½–1 teaspoon ground cumin
½–1 teaspoon salt
½ teaspoon sugar
2 tablespoons lemon juice
Small handful of fresh mint, chopped (optional)
Handful of unsalted peanuts, roughly chopped (optional)

Place the coriander, green chilli, garlic, ginger, cumin, salt, sugar and lemon juice in a small food processor or blender.

Add 1 tablespoon of water and blitz until smooth, adding more water as necessary to help the blitzing and adjust the consistency. The chutney should be thick but spoonable.

Add the mint and peanuts, if using, and pulse a few times to incorporate. The nuts will add texture without making the chutney too coarse.

Taste and adjust the seasoning, adding more salt, sugar or lemon juice as needed.

Store in a sealed container for up to a week, or up to 3 months in the freezer.

TAMARIND CHUTNEY

MAKES 250ML • PREP TIME: 20 MINUTES
COOK TIME: 12 MINUTES

100g (3½oz) tamarind block or pulp, soaked and strained
250ml (9fl oz) hot water
125–150g (4½–5½oz) jaggery or soft brown sugar
1 teaspoon roasted cumin powder
½ teaspoon mild chilli powder, such as Kashmiri
½ teaspoon salt
½ teaspoon black salt (kala namak)
½ teaspoon ground ginger, or 1-cm (½-inch) piece of fresh root ginger, grated

If using a tamarind block, soak it in the measured hot water for 15 minutes. Mash gently with a spoon, then strain through a fine sieve to remove fibres and seeds, reserving the water. If using tamarind pulp, simply measure and set aside.

Pour the prepared tamarind and reserved water into a small saucepan. Bring to a gentle simmer over a medium heat.

Stir in the jaggery or soft brown sugar until fully dissolved.

Add the roasted cumin powder, red chilli powder, both salts, and ginger. Mix well.

Let the mixture simmer gently for 10–15 minutes, stirring occasionally, until slightly thickened. The consistency should coat the back of a spoon but remain pourable.

Check for balance between sweet, sour and salty, adjusting as needed. This should be on the sweeter side. Remove from the heat and let cool slightly before using. Store in an airtight container in the fridge for up to a month, or in the freezer for up to 6 months.

MADHU'S GARLIC & CHILLI CHUTNEY

SERVES: 8 • PREP TIME: 10 MINUTES

100g (3½oz) red chilli powder (8–10 tablespoons)
6–8 garlic cloves, roughly chopped
1 teaspoon salt
4 tablespoons oil
1 teaspoon ground cumin (optional)

Using a blender, food processor, or mortar and pestle, combine the red chilli powder, garlic, salt, oil and cumin, if using, until smooth.

Add water, ½ teaspoon at a time, until the chutney reaches a thick and spoonable consistency. This should take around 5 minutes.

Check the seasoning and adjust the salt if necessary.

Store in a sealed container for up to 3 months, or in the freezer for up to 12 months.

HOMEMADE MANGO CHUTNEY

MAKES 300G • PREP TIME: 15 MINUTES
COOK TIME: 45 MINUTES

1 onion, very finely chopped
1 teaspoon black mustard seeds
1 teaspoon cumin seeds
2 garlic cloves, crushed or finely grated
2.5-cm (1-inch) piece of fresh root ginger, finely grated
2 large ripe mangoes, diced
150g (5½oz) light brown sugar
125ml (4fl oz) apple cider vinegar or white wine vinegar
1 teaspoon salt
½ teaspoon ground turmeric
½ teaspoon ground cumin
½ teaspoon chilli flakes

In a dry pan over a medium heat, toast the mustard and cumin seeds for 30–60 seconds, until fragrant and starting to pop.

Add the onion to the pan and cook, stirring frequently, for 5–7 minutes, until soft and translucent but not browned. Add the garlic and ginger and cook for 1 minute until aromatic.

Stir in the mango, brown sugar, vinegar, salt, turmeric, ground cumin and chilli flakes. Mix well to combine.

Reduce the heat to low and cook uncovered for 30–40 minutes, stirring every 5 minutes, until the chutney thickens to a glossy, jam-like consistency. Adjust the heat to maintain a gentle simmer.

Remove from the heat and spoon the hot chutney into sterilized jars, while still hot. The chutney will thicken more as it cools.

Let cool slightly, then seal while still warm.

SOUTH INDIAN COCONUT CHUTNEY

SERVES: 4 • PREP TIME: 10 MINUTES
COOK TIME: 5 MINUTES

85g (3oz) grated coconut, fresh or frozen and defrosted
2 tablespoons roasted chana dal (split chickpeas)
1 small green chilli (deseed if you want less heat)
1-cm (½-inch) piece of fresh root ginger
1 garlic clove, grated (optional)
2–3 tablespoons water (as needed)
Salt, to taste

FOR TEMPERING
1 tablespoon oil, preferably coconut
½ teaspoon mustard seeds
½ teaspoon urad dal (black lentils)
1 dried red chilli
6–8 fresh curry leaves
Pinch of asafoetida

Place the coconut, chana dal, green chilli, ginger, salt, garlic and 2 tablespoons of water in a blender or food processor. Blitz until smooth but still slightly textured. Add more water, a teaspoon at a time, if needed to reach your desired consistency.

Transfer the coconut mixture to a serving bowl. Taste and adjust the salt.

Heat the oil in a small pan over a medium heat. Add the mustard seeds and allow them to pop.

Add the urad dal and fry until lightly golden.

Add the dried red chilli, curry leaves, and asafoetida. Stir briefly until aromatic.

Pour the hot tempering immediately over the blended coconut chutney. Mix gently.

Adjust the thickness as needed: thicker for idli, slightly looser for dosa or a dip. Serve immediately.

Dosa-associates

SAMBAR

SERVES: 4–6 • PREP TIME: 15 MINUTES
COOK TIME: 30 MINUTES

100g (3½oz) split pea dal
¼ teaspoon ground turmeric
1 small carrot, chopped
1 small onion or 6–8 shallots, chopped
6–8 green beans
1 large tomato, chopped
Lemon-sized block of tamarind, soaked in 250ml (9fl oz) warm water for 15 minutes and strained
1½ tablespoons sambar powder (alternatively mix together: 2 teaspoons ground coriander, 1 teaspoon ground cumin, ½ teaspoon turmeric, ½–1 teaspoon mild or regular chilli powder, ½ teaspoon black pepper, ¼ teaspoon ground fenugreek, ½ teaspoon mustard powder)
Salt, to taste

FOR TEMPERING
2 teaspoons oil or ghee
½ teaspoon mustard seeds
½ teaspoon cumin seeds (optional)
2 dried red chillies
8–10 curry leaves
Pinch of asafoetida

Put the dal and turmeric in a medium pan and cook until soft. If using a pressure cooker, add 500ml (18fl oz) water and cook for 3–4 whistles.

Mash the dal until smooth and set aside.

In a separate pan, cook the carrot, onion and green beans with 500ml (18fl oz) water until just tender.

Add the cooked dal and their cooking water to the vegetables and combine. Stir in the tamarind, sambar powder (or spice mix), salt and tomato. Simmer gently for 10–12 minutes. The consistency should be pourable, not thick like dal. Adjust the water if necessary.

Prepare the tempering by heating the oil or ghee in a small pan, then adding the remaining ingredients. Fry until fragrant.

Pour the tempering over the sambar and serve immediately.

ANY VEG PICKLE

SERVES: 10–15 • PREP TIME: 20 MINUTES, PLUS 1 HOUR RESTING/SOFTENING
COOK TIME: 5 MINUTES

3 large carrots or other crunchy vegetables, such as radish, peeled and cut into thin batons
8–10 fresh green chillies, slit lengthways (deseed if you want less heat)
2 teaspoons salt
1 teaspoon ground turmeric
2 teaspoons yellow mustard seeds, coarsely crushed
1 teaspoon fenugreek seeds, lightly crushed
½ teaspoon asafoetida (optional, but traditional)
2 tablespoons lemon juice
1–2 teaspoons sugar (for a Gujarati touch)
3 tablespoons neutral oil

Wash and dry the carrots and chillies thoroughly. Excess moisture can dilute the seasoning and reduce the shelf life.

Place them in a large bowl and sprinkle with the salt and turmeric. Toss well and leave for 1 hour to soften slightly, then drain off any excess liquid.

Add the yellow mustard seeds or rai, fenugreek, asafoetida, if using, lemon juice and sugar. Mix thoroughly so everything is evenly coated.

Heat the oil in a small saucepan until just shimmering but not smoking. Allow it to cool for 1–2 minutes, then pour it over the vegetable mixture.

Mix well. Transfer to a clean, dry glass jar and press down gently then tighten the lid.

Leave at room temperature for about 24 hours before eating. The flavours deepen after 2–3 days. The pickle will keep in the refrigerator for up to 6 weeks.

MASALA CHILLI CRISP

MAKES 500ML • PREP TIME: 15 MINUTES (EXCLUDING MARINATION)
COOK TIME: 5 MINUTES

1 tablespoon chilli flakes
1 teaspoon sugar
Pinch of asafoetida
1 teaspoon cumin seeds
1 teaspoon mustard seeds
1 teaspoon coriander seeds
1 teaspoon fennel seeds
1 teaspoon nigella seeds (optional)
3–4 cloves
1 star anise
2.5-cm (1-inch) piece of cinnamon stick
4–5 green cardamom pods, lightly crushed
1 whole Kashmiri (mild) chilli
500ml (18fl oz) cold-pressed rapeseed oil
3–4 shallots or small onions, very finely sliced
8 garlic cloves, very finely sliced
10–15 curry leaves
1½ tablespoons soy sauce

Place everything up to and including the chilli in a large heatproof bowl. Set aside.

In a heavy-based saucepan, combine the rapeseed oil, shallots and garlic then place over a medium heat. Cook slowly, stirring regularly, until the shallots become deep golden and crisp and the garlic is lightly golden. This will take 15–20 minutes – don't rush it, as slow-frying builds sweetness and prevents bitterness.

Add the curry leaves during the final minute of cooking and allow them to crisp (they will splutter).

Once everything is deeply golden and aromatic, use a slotted spoon to transfer the shallots, garlic and curry to cool on a plate or tray – they will become very crisp as they cool.

Carefully pour the hot oil over the spice mixture in the bowl. The spices will sizzle and bloom instantly in the heat. Leave to sit for 10–15 minutes so the flavours infuse. When the oil has cooled to warm, stir in the soy sauce. Adjust the salt, sugar or chilli, if needed. Return the cooled shallots mixture to the infused oil.

Leave to cool completely before transferring to jars. The crisp should be fragrant, gently smoky, warmly spiced and deeply savoury, with crunchy shallots and garlic suspended in the golden oil.

This will keep for up to 6 months, out of the fridge.

INDEX

ABOUT THE AUTHOR

RIYA PATEL founded All the Aunties in 2024 with her brother-in-law Jack Newton, on a mission to spice up a food sector in desperate need of a refresh. Formerly a civil servant, Riya had a lightbulb moment about taking paneer – the high-protein, totally natural, Indian superfood – to a wider audience in a bid to create a standout paneer brand in health-food shops, supermarkets and beyond. The brand is already seeing huge growth, being picked up by major supermarkets, such as Tesco and Sainsbury's, as well as food retailers, from Whole Foods to Ocado. All the Aunties is also the recipient of several Great Taste awards.

www.alltheaunties.co.uk

@alltheauntiesuk

ACKNOWLEDGEMENTS

In writing this book, there have been a few fundamental learnings.

One: writing a cookbook is not easy (and certainly should not be considered a side project).

Two: squeezing recipes out of your family and translating them for the masses is even harder.

So it goes without saying that there are **so** many people to thank for bringing this book to life.

First, and most importantly, the Aunties. The women who loved me, fed me and taught me how to cook. They are the entire reason this business, and therefore this book, exists. Thank you.

Secondly, Jack, my brother-in-law and co-founder, without whom this business wouldn't be half of what it is. Literally. Thank you for taking a punt, coming on this journey with me, and for your constant belief. I'm very glad to call you my brother.

I also must thank the other member of the All The Aunties team, Charlie, who is also my flatmate (do you think we spend enough time together?!). Thank you for being my support system at midnight after cooking all day, and proofreading all these recipes. You're the best.

Of course, I have to thank my dad, Jay, and my sister, Tanvi, who both go above and beyond in their support for me. From buying me the laptop I wrote this book on, to ferrying me across London in the car when I hosted my first supper club and couldn't drive, all for a simple "thanks" in return. I owe you a hundred times over and hope one day I'm able to return even half the favours.

Thank you to the team who helped bring this book to life: Jo, Rosie, Jaz, Kris, Sonali, Davina and everyone else who helped prep a shot, fed back on recipes – even when there were sometimes whole ingredients missing – and were patient beyond belief with someone who really had no idea what she was doing. It's been the most surreal and wonderful experience working on this book, and I'm so, so grateful.

Lastly, thank you to our community of wonderful paneer consumers who tested these recipes over and over again. We started at the bottom, now we're here. You've made this book worthy of being one for every shelf.

Olivia Horne
Alan Tang
Megan Wilson
Jim McCarthy-Cheung
Eva Vidak
Archie Fletcher
Jasvinder Kaur
Hari Ashurst - Venn
Maya Oliver
Oliver Newland
Megan Prosser
Helen Murphy
Kayva Chauhan
Kosha Vyas
Nikhil Thandi
Priya Bowry (& Sudha Aunty!)
Varsha Mistry
Charlie & Bridget Calver